THANKSG COOKBOOK

Over 200 Wonderful and Delicious Thanksgiving Recipes

(Greatest Thanksgiving Cookbook of All Time)

Jason Hamilton

Published by Alex Howard

Thanksgiving Cookbook: Over 200 Wonderful and Delicious Thanksgiving Recipes (Greatest Thanksgiving Cookbook of All Time)

ISBN 978-1-989891-92-6

Legal & Disclaimer

The information contained in this book is not designed to replace or take the place of any form of medicine or professional medical advice. The information in this book has been provided for educational and entertainment purposes only.

Table of contents

Part 1

Chapter 1: Introduction to Keto Recipes for Thanksgiving

It's that time of year again! Thanksgiving signifies as the beginning of the holiday season. It is the time to bond with family, a moment of sharing and expressing gratitude. The most exciting part of Thanksgiving is having a huge feast. But what will you do if you are on a special diet? And you do not want to pack on more weight?

Avoid the holiday weight gain and start making those high-quality recipes and excellent nutrient-dense foods that taste amazing without gaining on the overuse of sugar. These mouthwatering recipes will give you loads of ideas to prepare and serve at your Thanksgiving celebrations.

I will assure that you will not be disappointed in every single recipe of this book because each one of them was formulated based on people's health and taste buds. Enjoy each page with detailed recipes that you and your family will surely enjoy during Thanksgiving.

I hope everyone will have a fantastic keto-friendly Thanksgiving day!

Chapter 2: Your Ultimate Guide to Keto Diet Thanksgiving Meals

Thanksgiving, this is the time of the year when everybody is busy. We have so much to do, decorate, shop, party plan, party hop, check your list twice, wrap presents, get presents, the whole works and then you try to add the food factor in on top of that. How can we enjoy the holiday season without depriving ourselves on the foods that we want? Can we have happy eating without taking in consideration that we are on this kind of diet? Well, stop worrying because there's a lot of delicious food out there that will not cause you any weights and these foods are Keto Diet Approved. This book will guide your holiday meal plan.

A Keto Diet is consists of roughly 75% fats, 20% protein, and 5% carbs, but you want to keep your net daily carbs below approximately 30 grams. In this book, we are going to prepare meals that are rich in fat, less in protein and carbohydrate.

Keto Thanksgiving: Tips and Tricks

How do we recognize that the food we are going to prepare during Thanksgiving is Keto friendly? Here are handful tips and tricks on how to enjoy eating even you are on a Keto Diet.

Technically there's a lot of artificially sweetened, low-carb ice cream-type crap that you can squeeze into the diet, but that stuff is garbage, So if you want that information to go somewhere else, let's start with the thing that you have to avoid altogether.

- Grains - that includes bread, pasta, quinoa, oatmeal, cookies; You've got to avoid these things at all costs.
- Starchy vegetables - those are things like potatoes, yams, off-the-menu.
- Milk - not only is milk generally not healthy, but it's also surprisingly high in carbs. One exception here is full-fat milk, which if you are going to drink, do it in small quantities.
- Legumes - This includes all beans, chickpeas, lentils, Not only are they high in carbs, but they're also notoriously awful for digestion.
- Vegetables - you have to be careful here as well. You want to focus on leafy, non-starchy, above the ground type vegetables.
- Fruits - those are off the menu as well. So no bananas, apples, mangos, nada. One exception here is berries, which are moderate carbs, thus if you do eat them, minimal quantities.
- Artificial sweeteners - If you need a sweetener stick to something natural like stevia, or monk fruit.
- Beer, wine, cocktails - Beer and wine are very high carb, technically, hard alcohol is empty calories,

meaning there's no carbs, no fat, no protein; so you can get away with it but in moderation.

Once again, every meal you want to be aiming for roughly ¾ healthy fats,¼ protein and as few carbs as possible. Let us use healthy fats. For cooking, you can use coconut oil, grass-fed butter, and ghee, and you can also use leftover grease from cooking certain meats like bacon. For salads, definitely olive oil. You can even eat things like chicken and pork chops, but keep in mind that they're deficient in fat and so if you do eat something like that, you want to eat it with more fat in conjunction. So you're eating chicken, you'll eat more avocado or some macadamia nuts to compensate. Keep all of these tips on your list, and you can never go wrong with your diet.

Chapter 3: 10 Keto Recipes To Make On Thanksgiving

Cauliflower Mac and Cheese Keto Recipe

Ingredients:

1 tbsp of butter
½ cup heavy whipping cream
2 oz cream cheese (or use different flavor cream cheese)
2 cups cheese (cheddar/mozzarella blend) - set aside ½ cup for top
2 12 oz bag cauliflower (thawed)
seasoning to taste (Salt, pepper, onion powder, garlic powder, cayenne pepper)
chicken broth (but not necessary)
green bean casserole

Procedure:

1. First, melt buttercream and cream cheese in a saucepan on medium-low heat. Once melted, add the cheese. Add the chicken broth and cauliflower.
2. Put the cheese sauce on top of cauliflower and stir to combine. If the cheese sauce becomes thick, it

means the cauliflower is cold. But it's okay; it will melt while in the oven.
3. Wait for about 30 mins. Get it out of the oven and let it sit for about ten mins before serve.

Low Carb Shrimp and Grits (3 servings)
Ingredients:

1 lb shrimp (peeled and deveined)
1 lb floret of cauliflower
4 oz pancetta or bacon (diced)
2 tbsp onion (diced)
1 tbsp garlic (minced)
½ c. scallions (chopped)
4 oz gouda cheese (shredded smoked)
3 tbsp butter
3 tbsp heavy whipping cream
lemon (squeeze)
salt and pepper

Procedure:

1. If the cauliflower is frozen, heat it on the microwave for 10 to 12 minutes and stir it occasionally. Mash the potato and add one tablespoon of butter, heavy whipping cream, and gouda cheese. Mix it well and season with salt and pepper. Keep warm.
2. Saute the bacon or pancetta on medium-low heat until crispy. Remove and then set aside. For the remaining bacon fat, add two tablespoons of butter

and cook the onions until lightly brown. Add garlic and stir for 30 seconds.

3. Cook the shrimp for approximately 8 to 10 minutes or until the shrimp get to cook. Remove from heat and mix it with the bacon or pancetta and scallions.
4. Serve the grits in a bowl and top it with the shrimp and sauce.

Roasted Bacon and Brussels Sprouts with Garlic Parmesan Cream Sauce

Ingredients:

For Brussels Sprouts:
6 bacon slices (cut of thick)
1.5 lbs brussels sprouts (cleaned and cut in half)
2 tbsp butter or ghee
1 tbsp onion flakes (minced)

For the Sauce:
½ cup heavy cream
½ cup parmesan cheese (grated)
3 cloves garlic (minced)
sea salt to taste
cracked black pepper (a generous amount)

Procedure:

For The Brussels Sprouts:
1. Cook the bacon until crispy on a large pan over medium heat. Remove the bacon from the pan, and set aside. Retain the drippings.
2. In the skillet, add butter to the bacon drippings. Melt the butter, add brussels sprouts and minced onion flakes.
3. Saute, occasionally tossing until the brussels sprouts are golden brown and crisp-tender. Add the bacon back to the pan and stir with the brussels sprouts.

For The Sauce:
1. Add heavy cream in a small saucepan over medium-high heat. Add Parmesan cheese, garlic, sea salt, and cracked black pepper.
2. Bring it to boil then adjust heat to low. Stirring occasionally, let simmer and thicken.
3. Pour over the roasted brussels sprouts.
4. Serve and enjoy!

Creole Shrimp and Eggplant Étouffée

Ingredients:

8x11 baking dish
¼ cup olive oil
1 pc eggplant (medium)
1 ½ tsp salt
¼ tsp cayenne
¼ tsp ground black pepper
½ cup green onions (chopped)
¼ cup bell peppers (chopped)
¼ cup celery (chopped)
½ lb medium shrimp
½ tsp thyme (dried)
½ tsp old bay
½ tsp garlic powder
1 ¾ cups vegetable stock
1 cup ground pork rinds (¼ cup for topping)
½ cup parmesan (grated) (¼ cup for topping)
4 ½ cups cauliflower (cooked, riced)

Procedure:

1. First, make sure that the shrimp are peeled and deveined. Cut the shrimp into thirds and place it in a small bowl. Season it with some garlic powder, thyme and old bay seasoning (mix to coat). Cover and put it on the refrigerator.

2. Cut the top and bottom of the eggplant. Dice the eggplant into about 1-inch pieces. Put it in the pan with medium-high heat and add ¼ cup of extra virgin oil. Add salt, ground black pepper and a pinch of cayenne pepper. Saute for 2 to 3 mins to make the eggplant soften a bit. Add ½ cup of chopped green onions, celery, green bell pepper and saute for an additional 3 minutes.
3. Now, add the shrimp and continue to cook until it turns into pink. Add some vegetable stock and cook for another four minutes.
4. Turn the heat off and then add one cup of ground pork rinds and freshly grated parmesan cheese. Stir until thickened. Pour the mixture into the casserole and top it with a few more cheese and ground pork rinds. Put it in the preheated oven for 30 minutes until browned. Once done, remove it in the oven and let it cool for 15 minutes.
5. Etouffée usually serves with rice, but since we are preparing a keto friendly meal, we'll be using a steamed riced cauliflower. Put the cooked rice cauliflower to a plate, pour in the shrimp and eggplant, garnish with a bit of dried parsley and serve!

Bell Pepper Nachos

Ingredients:

3 pcs bell peppers (1 each color, sliced into nacho size pieces)

1 tbsp of oil
1 lb ground beef
1 ½ tbsp taco seasoning
½ cup salsa (divided)
8 oz cheddar cheese (grated)
4 oz can black olives
½ cup guacamole
¼ cup sour cream

Procedure:

1. Start to preheat the oven to 350 degrees. Place the oven rack in the middle position and line a large baking sheet with parchment pepper.
2. Heat 1 tbsp oil into the medium heat pan. Add the ground beef and taco seasoning, cook for about 8 to 10 minutes.
3. Place the bell pepper slices in the oven for 5 minutes. Remove it from the oven and top it with meat mixture, salsa, cheese, and other toppings you want to be heated. Place it again into the oven and bake until the cheese melts. Remove from the oven and cool down before serving.
4. Serve the guacamole and sour cream into a separate container, send with bell pepper nachos.

Keto Cauliflower Risotto & Salmon Meal
Ingredients:

Salmon and asparagus Ingredients (3 servings):

18 oz salmon
1 bundle asparagus
spray olive oil

Seasonings:
2 tsp olive oil
2 tsp herb seasoning (no/low sodium)
1 tsp smoked paprika
salt & pepper

Risotto Ingredients (5 servings):
1 medium cauliflower (about 3.5 cups of raw cauliflower "rice")
1 ½ cup chopped portobello mushrooms (optional)
2 tbsp extra virgin olive oil
2 cloves garlic (chopped)
8 oz coconut cream (vegan, unsweetened)
½ cup parmesan cheese (shredded)
⅓ cup chicken broth

Seasonings:
1 tbsp rosemary (fresh or dried)
2 tsp thyme (fresh or dried)
salt & pepper
red pepper

Procedure:

1. Set the oven to 420° F
2. Chop the bottom end of the asparagus

3. Season raw salmon fillet with olive oil, herb seasoning, smoked paprika, and salt and pepper. Place the salmon on a tray beside the asparagus spears.
4. Spray the asparagus with olive oil and add few pinches of salt, pepper, red pepper and bake it for 15 to 20 minutes
5. Remove the florets of the cauliflower and place the florets in a blender until you create rice-like chunks.
6. Set a nonstick pan on medium-high heat and add olive oil. Put the chopped garlic and cook for about 2 minutes (do not burn the garlic).
7. Now, put the portobello mushroom with seasonings in the pan and cook for about 3 to 5 minutes.
8. Put in the cauliflower rice to the pan and cook it for about 2 to 3 minutes.
9. Pour in the coconut cream, chicken broth, parmesan cheese.
10. Reduce the heat to low-medium, stir and bring the mixture to a simmer.
11. Place the pan in heat and allow it to cook for about 15 minutes until you get a creamy consistency much like risotto.
12. Prepare the meal with salmon, asparagus and creamy cauliflower risotto.

Broccoli & Chicken Stir Fry Recipe

Ingredients:

500 grams pound of chicken thighs

1 tbsp sesame oil
1 broccoli (whole head chopped into thin slice)
salt
3 cloves garlic (chopped)
2 tbsp tamari (fermented soy)
ginger or seasoning (optional)

Procedure:

1. Use and heat a large frying pan and add a large amount tablespoon of sesame oil.
2. Once hot, add the chicken on the frying pan with oil.
3. Add a bit of salt, stir and get the sesame flavor onto the chicken.
4. Add a couple of chopped garlic cloves for some extra flavor. Wait until the chicken turns a little brown.
5. Set aside and add in the broccoli.
6. Put in some tamari. It's recommended to use tamari instead of soy sauce because it is a fermented soy sauce that is more than enough to add flavor.
7. Mix everything all together and cook until the broccoli and chicken is all cooked. Serve.

Keto Teriyaki Steak

Ingredients:

33 oz ribeye steak
2 tbsp garlic (cut into thin slices)
¼ cup grapeseed oil
2 tbsp butter
1 tsp salt
1 tsp black pepper
¼ cup keto teriyaki sauce
¼ cup of keto teriyaki glaze (with sesame seeds)

Procedure:

1. Combine and mix the teriyaki sauce and glaze in a cup. Stir and set aside.
2. Apply pepper and salt to the ribeye steak and set aside
3. Take a large pan and set it over to a medium high temperature. Add the grapeseed oil and butter. Stir until coat the entire bottom of the pan. Add the garlic to the pan until crispy. Get the garlic out of the oil and place into a small dish. Set aside.
4. Place the steak on the frying pan and sear the meat to a golden brown both sides.
5. Turn the heat down and pour half of the teriyaki over the steak. Flip until it applies to the rest of the teriyaki sauce.
6. Fry until you get the cook you want (rare, medium-rare, medium) whatever you like

7. Remove the pan and place the steak on a plate and rest for at least 10 minutes before cutting into strips.

Best Ever Chicken Bake Recipe

Ingredients:

2 kg chicken drumsticks (legs)
1 cup pizza/pasta sauce
garlic cloves (peeled)
salt and pepper to taste
grated cheese

Procedure:

1. Fill the ovenproof dish with chicken.
2. Pour over the sauce and garlic cloves on the chicken.
3. Add extra seasoning of your choice and stir to combine.
4. Place the dish on the preheated oven (180C/350F) for 30 to 45 minutes.
5. After 45 minutes, remove it from the oven and flip the chicken, sprinkle over the grated cheese and return it on the oven for another 30 minutes until cooked. Serve.

Cauliflower Mashed Potato

Ingredients:

1 head of cauliflower (about 800g)
100 ml double heavy cream
50g salted butter
1 cup chicken broth
2 chicken stock cubes
herbs and spices

Procedure:

1. Cut the cauliflower head and get the florets out. Just a tip, get rid of as much stalk as you can that where the carbs are.
2. Put the cauliflower florets in a pot with 1 cup of water.
3. Add 1 to 2 chicken stock cubes to the water.
4. Set the pot on manual, high pressure for about 7 minutes.
5. Transfer the cauliflower into a bowl and use a sieve to drain.
6. Add 100ml of double heavy cream, some herbs, and spices to taste.
7. Cauliflower should be soft that you can mash it with a regular masher or blender. Serve.

Chapter 4: Keto Thanksgiving Recipe You'll Surely Love

Cauliflower Mash

Ingredients:

1 head cauliflower (medium)
3 oz butter
1 tsp salt
½ tsp pepper

Procedure:

1. Boil water to a large pot.
2. Cut the cauliflower into evenly sized florets.
3. Add the cauliflower to the boiling water. Cook it for 5-8 minutes until the cauliflower is tender.
4. Drain the cauliflower well and return it to the warm pot.
5. Add the butter, salt, and pepper.
6. Put the cauliflower to a blender with a good stick blender until there are no lumps.
7. Let the mash to sit and rest for 3 minutes and then blend a second time. This rest and blend step make the cauliflower extra smooth and creamy.
8. Serve and enjoy.

Easy Low Carb Pumpkin Cheesecake Pie

Ingredients

Crust:
1 ¾ cups almond flour
½ tsp cinnamon
1 ½ tbsp all-purpose flour
1 stick butter (melted)

Filling:
⅓ cup all purpose flour
16 oz cream cheese
½ tsp vanilla extract
⅔ cup pumpkin puree
2 large eggs
½ tsp cinnamon
¼ tsp nutmeg
⅛ tsp allspice

Procedure:

Crust:
1. Mix almond flour, cinnamon, and sweetener in 9-inch pie pan.
2. Stir in melted butter.
3. Press the mixture down into pie pan with hands.

Filling:

1. Put the ingredients in a large mixing bowl, combine cream cheese, sweetener, and vanilla with electric mixer until smooth. Use a food processor to mix well all the ingredients for the filling.
2. Blend in the pumpkin, eggs, cinnamon, nutmeg, and allspice until well combined.
3. Pour pumpkin cheesecake filling into prepared crust. Bake for about 35-40 minutes at 350ºF.
4. Allow cheesecake to cool on a rack. Chill in the refrigerator for an overnight before serving.

Sugar-Free Cranberry Sauce

Ingredients:

12 oz whole cranberries (fresh or frozen)
1 cup powdered erythritol sweetener
1 cup water
1 tbsp fresh orange zest (about 1 orange)

Procedure:

1. If using granulated erythritol, blend it in a small blender for a few seconds until it reaches a powdered consistency.
2. Add erythritol and water to a pan. Simmer over medium-high heat, stirring occasionally.
3. Add cranberries to the pan, stir with the liquid. Cook until it boils, and reduce to medium heat.
4. Cook the cranberries until split open and the sauce reaches your desired consistency, about 10 to 15 minutes, stirring occasionally.
5. Add orange zest, stir well for a minute. Serve immediately while warm.

Keto Turkey Gravy

Ingredients:

½ tsp glucomannan powder
2 cups turkey broth
4 oz butter
2 tbsp parsley seasoning
1 tsp ground rosemary seasoning
salt and pepper to taste

Procedure:

1. Melt the butter in a small pan. Add two cups of turkey broth.
2. Add the seasonings to the mixture.
3. Add ½ tsp of Glucomannan Powder to the gravy once it's warm. Stir to mix it in until it has completely dissolved.
4. Set aside the gravy for about 5 minutes. Wait until it thickens. Use the same amount of Glucomannan powder even if you decide to make this recipe and leave out the butter. I've tried it both ways, and it works both ways. Just remember, a small amount of this powder goes a long way.

Sugar-Free Pecan Pie

Ingredients:

Crust:
1 ½ cups almond flour
¼ cup swerve sweetener
¼ tsp salt
¼ cup butter melted

Filling:
1 recipe almond flour pie crust
¾ cup butter
½ cup swerve brown
½ cup bocha sweet
1 ½ tsp vanilla extract or maple extract
¼ tsp salt
3 large eggs
1 ½ cups pecan halves

Procedure:

Crust:
1. Whisk together almond flour, sweetener, and salt in a medium bowl. Stir in melted butter until dough comes along and resembles coarse crumbs.
2. Put it into a pie plate (can be glass or ceramic). Press tightly with fingers into the bottom and up sides. Use a flat-bottomed glass or measuring cup to even out the bottom. Before baking, prick all over with a fork.

3. Preheat the oven at 325 F to bake unfilled. Bake for about 20 minutes until edges reach golden brown.
4. To bake a filled pie, pre-bake 10-12 minutes before adding fillings. Cover with foil to avoid the over-browning of the edges.
5. For a savory pie crust, leave out the sweetener, use ½ tsp salt, and add ½ tsp garlic powder.

Filling:
1. Follow the directions in preparing pie crust and bake at 325 F for 10 minutes. Take it out and let cool while making the filling.
2. Over low heat, melt the butter with the two sweeteners in a large saucepan, stirring until the sweeteners have dissolved for about 2 minutes. Remove from heat and then mix in the vanilla extract and salt.
3. Make sure the syrup isn't too hot and then whisk in the eggs.
4. Place the pecans in the cooled crust and pour the filling over the top. Return to the oven and bake 45 to 50 minutes.
5. Remember: If the crust is browning too quickly, cover the pie with aluminum foil, shiny side up, about halfway through the baking time. Let cool completely before serving.

Oven Roasted Turkey Legs

Ingredients:

2 turkey legs (medium)
2 tbsp duck fat
2 tsp salt
½ tsp pepper
¼ tsp cayenne pepper
½ tsp onion powder
½ tsp garlic powder
½ tsp dried thyme
½ tsp ancho chili powder
1 tsp liquid smoke
1 tsp worcestershire

Procedure:

1. Put all dry spices in a small bowl and mix. Then, add wet ingredients and mix into a rub.
2. Dry turkey legs completely with paper towels. Then, rub turkey legs well with seasoning.
3. Preheat oven to 350 F. Brings 2 tbsp of fat to medium-high heat in a cast iron skillet. Add turkey legs into the pan when the oil starts to smoke and sear on each side for 1-2 minutes.
4. Put in the oven with 350 F temperature for 50 to 60 minutes or until cooked.
5. Take turkey out from the oven and let rest for a few minutes.
6. Serve with side dish and enjoy the holiday meal!

Low Carb Paleo Cauliflower Stuffing

Ingredients:

1 large head cauliflower (cut into small florets)
1 large onion (sliced)
¼ cup celery (chopped thinly)
2 cloves minced garlic
¼ cup olive oil
½ tsp poultry seasoning
½ tsp dried thyme
½ tsp ground sage
1 tsp sea salt
¼ tsp black pepper
2 tbsp parsley (freshly chopped)
¼ cup pecans (chopped)

Procedure:

1. Preheat oven at 450 degrees F. Line a baking sheet with parchment paper or line with foil and grease well.
2. Combine the chopped cauliflower, onions, celery, and garlic in a large bowl. Season with olive oil, poultry seasoning, sage, thyme, sea salt, and black pepper.
3. Apply the mixture in a single layer on the lined baking sheet. Cook in the oven for about 15 minutes. Wait until the onions are soft and cauliflower is starting to brown a little.

4. In a pan add the fresh parsley and pecans, and mix the ingredients. Roast for 10-15 more minutes, wait until the pecans are lightly toasted, cauliflower is brown, and onions are starting to caramelize.

Deviled Eggs

Ingredients:

Recipe for the Base:
12 large eggs hard-boiled (peeled and sliced in half)
½ mayonnaise
½ tsp sea salt

Classic Deviled Eggs:
2 tsp dijon mustard
1 ½ tsp vinegar
⅛ tsp black pepper (freshly cracked)
¼ tsp paprika (plus more for garnish)
parsley for garnish (chopped chives)

Smoked Salmon:
2 tsp dijon mustard
3 tbsp softened cream cheese
2 tsp fresh lemon juice
⅛ tsp black pepper (freshly cracked)
½ sp dill (plus more garnish)
1 tbsp capers (finely chopped)
5 tbsp minced smoked salmon (plus more for garnish)

Broccoli & Cheese:
2 tsp dijon mustard
1 ½ tsp vinegar
⅛ tsp black pepper (cracked)
⅓ c broccoli (chopped)
⅓ c grated cheddar cheese (plus more for garnish)

Buffalo Chicken:
⅓ c buffalo sauce
2 tbsps plain full fat greek yogurt
⅛ tsp black pepper (freshly cracked)
½ c cooked chicken (chopped)
⅓ c blue cheese (crumbled)

Spicy Chili:
4 tsps chili garlic sauce (plus more for garnish)
2 tsps lime juice
½ tsp paprika-smoked (plus more for sprinkling)
⅛ tsp black pepper (freshly cracked)

Chipotle and Salsa:
2 tsps lime juice
⅛ black pepper (freshly cracked)
1 tbsp canned chipotle chiles (chopped)
3 tbsps chunky salsa drained (plus more for garnish)

Avocado:
1 ½ ripe avocado (mashed)
1 tsp dijon mustard
3 tsps lime juice (fresh)
1 tsp dried tarragon (plus more for Garnish)
⅛ tsp black pepper (freshly cracked)
diced green peppers for Garnish

Bacon and Cheese:
2 tsps dijon mustard

1 ½ tsp vinegar
⅛ tsp black pepper (cracked)
⅓ c chopped bacon (plus more for Garnish)
⅓ c grated cheddar cheese (plus more for Garnish)

Sun-Dried Tomato:
2 tsps dijon mustard
1 ½ tsp vinegar
⅛ tsp black pepper (freshly cracked)
3 tbsp finely chopped sun-dried tomatoes (plus more for garnish)
⅓ c feta crumbled (plus more for garnish)
1 tbsp chopped parsley (plus more for garnish)

SouthWestern:
2 tsps dijon mustard
2 tsp chipotle or tabasco hot sauce
1 ½ tsp lime juice
½ tsp cumin
1 tsps smoked paprika
2 tbsp finely chopped jalapeno peppers (plus more for garnish)
¼ c grated cheddar cheese (plus more for garnish)
¼ c chopped red bell pepper (plus more for garnish)

Ham & Cheddar Cheese:
2 tsps dijon mustard
1 ½ tsp vinegar
⅛ tsp cracked black pepper
⅓ c chopped ham (plus more for garnish)

⅓ c grated cheddar (plus more for garnish)

Dill Pickle:
2 tsp dijon mustard
1 tbsp dill pickle juice
⅛ tsp black pepper (freshly cracked)
2 tsp fresh dill minced (plus more for garnish)
2 tbsp dill pickles (minced)
1 tbsp fresh dill (minced)

Procedure:

Base Recipe:
1. In eggs in half lengthwise slice the eggs and separate the egg yolks in a large bowl. Mash into a crumble with a fork.
2. Add Mayonnaise and salt.

Classic Deviled Eggs:
1. Add Mustard, Vinegar and black pepper. Mash until combined and smooth.
2. Spoon the yolk mixture into egg white halves.
3. Sprinkle the top with paprika and garnish with chives and parsley (if desired).

Smoked Salmon:
1. Add cream cheese, mustard, lemon juice, dill, and black pepper. Mash until combined and smooth. Stir in capers and smoked salmon.
2. Spoon the filling into each egg white.

3. Sprinkle on top the desired amount of smoked salmon pieces and dill.

Broccoli and Cheese:
1. Add vinegar, mustard, and black pepper. Mash until completely smooth. Stir in broccoli and cheese.
2. Spoon yolk filling into each egg white.
3. Garnish with more cheese.

Buffalo Chicken:
1. Add greek yogurt, buffalo sauce, and black pepper. Mash until combined and smooth. Stir in chicken and cheese.
2. Spoon or pipe yolk filling into each white.
3. Glaze with more hot sauce and crumbled cheese.

Spicy Chili:
1. Add lime juice, chili sauce, lime juice, smoked paprika, and black pepper. Mash until combined and smooth.
2. Spoon filling into each egg white.
3. Glaze with more hot sauce and a sprinkle of paprika.

Chipotle and Salsa:
1. Add lime juice and black pepper. Mash until combined and smooth. Stir in chipotles and salsa
2. Spoon the filling into each egg white. Garnish with more salsa.

Avocado:

1. Mash the avocado. Add lime juice, tarragon, mustard, and black pepper. Mash until combined and smooth.
2. Scoop the filling into each egg white. Garnish with green peppers and tarragon, if desired.

Bacon and Cheese:
1. Add vinegar, mustard, and black pepper. Mash until completely smooth. Stir in ham and cheese.
2. Spoon yolk filling into each egg white.
3. Garnish with more bacon and cheese.

Sun-Dried Tomato:
1. Add vinegar, mustard, and black pepper. Mash until completely smooth. Stir in sun-dried tomato, cheese, and parsley.
2. Spoon yolk filling into each egg white.
3. Glaze with more sun-dried tomatoes, cheese, and parsley.

Southwestern:
1. Add hot sauce, lime juice, mustard, cumin, and paprika. Mash until smooth. Stir in Jalapenos red bell pepper and cheese.
2. Spoon yolk filling into each egg white.
3. Garnish with chopped jalapenos and paprika.

Ham and Cheddar:
1. Add vinegar, mustard, and black pepper. Mash until completely smooth. Stir in ham and cheese.

2. Spoon yolk filling into each egg white.
3. Garnish with more ham and cheese.

Dill Pickle:
1. Add pickle juice, dill, mustard, and black pepper. Mash until completely smooth. Stir in chopped pickles.
2. Spoon yolk filling into each egg white.
3. Garnish with pickle slices and dill.

Chapter 5: Delectable Keto Holiday Recipes

Extremely Creamy Eggnog

Ingredients:

6 egg yolks
½-¾ cup swerve or xylitol
2 cups almond milk (unsweetened)
2 cups heavy cream
1 cinnamon stick
1 tsp nutmeg (freshly grated)
2 tsp vanilla extract
1 cup dark rum or bourbon to taste

Procedure:

1. Add egg yolks and put to a large bowl, and using a whisk or an electric mixer, beat them until light, fluffy, and all the sweetener dissolve completely. Set aside.
2. Add heavy cream, almond milk, cinnamon, and nutmeg to a medium saucepan and simmer, stir it often. Take out from heat and gradually temper the hot mixture into the egg and sugar mixture. Tempering means adding the warm milk little by

little to your egg mixture while whisking constantly, so your eggs don't curdle.

3. Put back all the ingredients to the saucepan. Over medium to low heat cook for about 8-10 minutes, or until your mixture reaches 160°F. Remove from the heat and filter into a medium mixing bowl. To taste, mix in vanilla and liquor of choice. To chill place in the refrigerator and cover.

4. Chilling will continue the eggnog to thicken. Give it a good stir before serving.

Pumpkin Spice Latte

Ingredients:

2 tbsp pumpkin (blended)
½ tsp pumpkin spice mix
1-2 tbsp golden erythritol (or sweetener of choice to taste)
1 tbsp vanilla extract
240 ml almond milk
1 tbsp coconut milk (full-fat)
2 shots espresso

To Garnish:
whipped cream (homemade)
pumpkin spice mix

Procedure:

1. Heat blended pumpkin and pumpkin pie spice in a small saucepan over medium heat. Stir constantly for 2 to 3 minutes, until fragrant and cooked.
2. Stir in sweetener of choice, mixing until just combined. Pour in milk, and simmer until warm. Observe that it doesn't boil over! Remove from heat.
3. Whisk until light and frothy and add vanilla extract, 30 seconds to a minute. Refrigerate the pumpkin spice mix for 4-5 days at this point.
4. Pour espresso in a mug. Add the pumpkin spiced milk. You can also alternatively add in some MCT

and grass-fed butter at the end and blend it all with a blender. Add whipped cream on top and a touch of pumpkin pie spice.

Flakey Pie Crust

Ingredients:

96 g almond flour
40 g coconut flour
½ tsp xanthan gum
¼ tsp kosher salt
½ tsp lemon or orange zest
100 g unsalted grass-fed butter cold
55 g cream cheese cold
1 egg lightly beaten
2 tsp apple cider vinegar
egg wash optional (for a glossy finish)

Procedure:

1. Add coconut flour, almond flour, xanthan gum, salt and zest to a food processor and pulse until evenly combined.
2. Add butter and cream cheese and wait for a few seconds until crumbly. Add in vinegar and egg and pulse until the dough begins to come together (but stop before it forms into a ball). Make sure not to over-process the dough just like with any pastry dough. It should resemble coarse breadcrumbs rather than cookie dough.
3. Wrap the dough onto cling film and pat into a round.
4. Refrigerate it for one hour or even up to 3 days.

5. Roll out dough between parchment paper. You need to work fast and in cold conditions because it is more fragile than regular pie crust. Patch up any cracks that occur by cramping the dough together. If the crust becomes unmanageable, pop it in the freezer for 5-10 minutes before carrying on.
6. Once shaped, pop it in the freezer for 10-15 minutes before baking. Brush with egg white for a glossy finish.
7. Bake at 390°F for 10-12 minutes if making something small such as crackers. And up to 30 minutes for empanadas and such. Always keep an eye on it, as grain-free flours tend to brown suddenly rather than gradually.

Creamy Baked Brie

Ingredients:

For Pie Crust:
1 batch gluten-free & keto pie crust

For the Brie Filling
1 7-inch wheel brie cheese
⅓ cup pecans (roughly chopped)
1 tsp thyme
¼ tsp garlic powder

Procedure:

1. 1. Preheat oven to 350°F. Line a baking tray with parchment paper.
2. 2. Flatten pastry dough in between two sheets of parchment paper, lightly sprinkle with coconut flour as needed. Cut depending on the size of your brie. Bake the trimmings into crackers.
3. 3. Spread out pecans, garlic powder, and thyme in the center of the pie crust. Place brie wheel on top.
4. 4. Brush edges with egg wash and folds around the wheel, trimming excess dough as needed. If any breakage occurs, patch it up by pressing the dough together, or adding a trimming if need be. If the dough becomes unmanageable, immediately place it in the freezer for 10 minutes before carrying on.
5. 5. Place wrapped brie wheel onto a prepared baking tray and freeze for at least 10 minutes (or

overnight) before baking. Brush with egg white and bake for 27-30 minutes, until golden. Always check to avoid excessive browning after minute 15-17, as coconut flour can brown too quickly. Place aluminum foil to slow excessive the browning if needed.

6. 6. Let it sit for about 10 minutes before serving; otherwise, the melted brie will ooze right out!

Baked Brie & Cranberry Festive Cups

Ingredients:

For the Dough:
96 g almond flour
24 g coconut flour
2 tsp xanthan gum
1 tsp baking powder
⅛ to ¼ teaspoon kosher salt (depending on whether sweet or savory)
2 tsp apple cider vinegar
1 egg (lightly beaten)
3 tsp water

For Keto Brie Cranberry Filling:
1 5-inch wheel brie cheese (diced)
40 g pecans (chopped)
1 tbsp rosemary (finely minced)
100 g keto cranberry (relish)

Procedure:

For the Dough:
1. Add coconut flour, almond flour, baking powder, xanthan gum, and salt to food processor. Wait until thoroughly combined.
2. Add apple cider vinegar while the food processor is running. Pour the egg when distributed evenly. Add water. Once the dough forms into a ball, turn off the food processor. The dough will be sticky to touch.

3. Wrap dough in cling film. Let it rest in the plastic for a minute or two. Allow dough to rest for another 10 minutes.
4. Divide the dough into eight 1" balls (26g a piece). Roll out between two sheets of parchment with a rolling pin. Trim edges if not satisfied with the presentation.
5. Preheat oven to 350°F.
6. Put pastry rounds into a muffin tray. Fill with brie, cranberry relish, rosemary, pecans, and brie again. Finalize with freshly ground black pepper to taste.
7. Bake for 10-16 minutes until pastry is golden and cheese melted. Always check on them, as coconut flour tends to brown quickly. Serve right away.
8. These are best served warm and straight from the oven.
9. Remember that you can assemble the cups a day before, wrap the muffin tray with cling film. Bake straight from the fridge as needed.

Sweet 'N Tangy Cranberry Relish

Ingredients:

90 ml white wine vinegar
8-12 tbsp swerve or xylitol (to taste)
50 g shallot (very finely minced)
1 rosemary spring (very finely chopped)
400 g cranberries

Procedure:

1. Heat a saucepan over medium/low heat, add vinegar and dissolve the sweetener in it for about 1 to 2 minutes. Add cranberries, shallot, and rosemary. Lower heat to low and cover. Simmer for 20-25 minutes. Stir often until thick and syrupy.
2. Feel free to taste it and adjust sweetness as needed.

Parmesan Keto Roasted Radishes

Ingredients:

2 bunches small to medium radishes (sliced)
2 tbsp extra virgin olive oil
2 tsp thyme (fresh or dried)
flakey sea salt to taste
black pepper (freshly ground to taste)
¼ cup parmesan cheese (freshly grated)

Procedure:

1. Preheat oven to 400°F. Brush a baking dish or surround the tray with olive oil.
2. Add radishes to a baking dish. Drizzle with olive oil, thyme, and season with salt and freshly ground black pepper to taste. Roast for 45 minutes until crisp and golden, tossing them about halfway through.
3. Sprinkle Parmesan cheese on top and roast for 5 more minutes. Serve right away.

Lemon & Parmesan Roasted Asparagus

Ingredients:

400 g asparagus (trimmed)
2 tbsp extra virgin olive oil
2 cloves garlic (ran through a press)
25 g parmesan cheese (freshly grated)
1 lemon (very thinly sliced)
kosher salt to taste
black pepper to taste (freshly ground)
parmesan (thinly sliced to serve)

Procedure:

1. Preheat oven to 400°F.
2. In a baking tray place trimmed asparagus. Sprinkle with olive oil and rub thoroughly with garlic. Drizzle Parmesan cheese, arrange lemon slices on top, and season with salt and freshly ground black pepper to taste.
3. Oven roast for 20 minutes. Serve straight away with more Parmesan, to taste.

Grain Free & Keto Graham Crackers

Ingredients:

192 g almond flour
½ tsp xanthan gum
¼ tsp kosher salt
½ tsp baking soda
1 tsp ground cinnamon
80 g grass-fed butter (at room temperature)
96 g golden erythritol
1 egg

Procedure:

1. Add baking soda, almond flour, xanthan gum, salt, and cinnamon to a medium bowl. Whisk until thoroughly combined and set aside.
2. Put cream butter in a large bowl with an electric mixer and beat for 2 to 3 minutes. Add in sweetener, continue to beat until light and fluffy and much of the sweetener has dissolved.
3. Add in egg, mixing until just incorporated. The mixture will appear slightly 'broken.'
4. Set mixer on low, add in half of your flour mixture. Mix until well combined.
5. Wrap the dough with cling film. Place the cookie dough in the refrigerator for at least one hour and up to 3 days.
6. Preheat oven to 350°F/180°C.

7. Flatten the dough using a rolling pin between two pieces of parchment paper until nice and thin. Using a pastry cutter, cut dough lengthwise and then crosswise into squares. Prick each piece with a fork (optional).
8. Transfer keto graham crackers on parchment paper to a baking sheet. Before baking, place in the freezer for about 10 minutes. The molded dough can be frozen for up to 3 months and baked straight from the fridge (adding 2-3 minutes more to the baking time).
9. Bake for 8-12 minutes, until fully golden. Watch out for your crackers, and if you like them more crispy, you'll have to adjust the baking time until deep golden.
10. Allow cooling for ten minutes before transferring to a cooling rack. Allow cooling completely, as they'll continue to crunch up (this may take a few hours for the sweetener to harden up again!).
11. Store in a sealed cookie jar for up to 5 days.

Pumpkin Cheesecake Ice Cream

Ingredients:

For Keto Pumpkin Cheesecake Ice Cream:
225 g pumpkin (blended)
1 ½ tsp pumpkin pie spice (homemade)
1 13.5 oz can coconut milk (full-fat)
135-150 g xylitol
¼ tsp kosher salt
¼ tsp xanthan gum
2 tsp vanilla extract
225g cream cheese (softened)
240 g sour cream (whipped)

For No bake Graham Cracker Crumbs (optional)
96 g almond flour
2-4 tbsp powdered xylitol (or sweetener of choice to taste)
½ tsp cinnamon
⅛ tsp kosher salt
28 g grass-fed butter (unsalted)

Procedure:

For Pumpkin Cheesecake Ice Cream:
1. Add blended pumpkin and pumpkin pie spice to a saucepan over medium heat. Cook, constantly stirring, for 3-5 minutes until cooked, fragrant, and deeper orange (but not brown!).

2. Pour in xylitol, coconut milk, salt, and mix well. Cook until the xylitol liquefies and everything is well combined.
3. Sprinkle xanthan gum little by little and stir until thoroughly combined. It will have some air bubbles, but be sure to check there are no lumps. Any lumps resolved by mixing with an immersion blender.
4. Put the mixture to a bowl, stir in vanilla extract, cover with a layer of cling film laid directly over the dough and allowed the mixture to cool completely. The texture will be thick and jelly-like.
5. In a large mixing bowl pour cream cheese and pumpkin mixture. Whisk until the cream cheese is thoroughly blended. To do this faster, use an electric whisk (or mixer/immersion blender), but also doable by hand.
6. Mix in whipped sour and transfer to a sealable container. Place in the freezer for 5-6 hours. 15 minutes before serving, take the ice cream out from the fridge and scoop away.
7. Or blend in an ice cream maker following the manufacturer's instructions for about 15 minutes. For the ice cream to be firmer, freeze in the covered container for one to two hours.
8. Fold the graham crackers or crumbs once the ice cream is semi-hard.

For Graham Cracker Crumbs (Optional):
1. Toast the almond lightly flour in a skillet or pan over medium heat, until fully golden and fragrant (2-4

minutes). Feel free to taste it for a much better result.

2. In a medium bowl transfer the toasted almond and add cinnamon, sweetener, and salt. Add in butter and mix until well mixed. Using your fingertips form them into clumps, transfer to a plate and let it sit. Place it on the freezer for 15-20 minutes before folding into the ice cream.

Pumpkin Spice Latte Muffins

Ingredients:

For the Keto Pumpkin Spice Latte Muffins:
64 g almond flour
21 g coconut flour
1 tbsp psyllium husk
1 tsp pumpkin pie spice
½ tsp xanthan gum
¼ tsp kosher salt
½ tsp baking powder
½ tsp baking soda
2 eggs (yolks & whites separated)
⅓ cup golden erythritol to taste
1 tsp vanilla extract
1 tsp apple cider vinegar
57 g unsalted grass-fed butter melted (slightly cooled)
60 ml espresso about 2 shots (cooled)

For the Pumpkin Filling (optional):
60 g pumpkin puree
56 g cream cheese
1 tbsp erythritol or xylitol
1 tsp vanilla extract
½ tsp pumpkin pie spice

For the Frosting (optional):
½ cream cheese buttercream frosting (optional)

For the Almond Streusel (optional):

64 g almond flour

21 g coconut flour

¾ tsp pumpkin pie spice

1 tbsp erythritol

¼ tsp kosher salt

42 g unsalted grass-fed butter

33 g pecans

Procedure:

For the Keto Pumpkin Spice Latte Muffins:

1. Whip the filling first if you want to have muffin filling. Preheat oven to 350°F. Grease and dust a muffin tray with coconut flour.
2. Mix in a medium bowl almond flour, coconut flour, psyllium husk, pumpkin pie spice, xanthan gum, baking powder, baking soda, and salt. Set aside.
3. Beat egg yolks with sweetener in a large bowl with an electric mixer on medium speed until pale and fluffy for 1 to minutes.
4. Combine melted butter, vanilla extract, and vinegar. Slowly add flour mixture, alternating with coffee and beating until just incorporated. Set aside.
5. Beat egg wash until soft peaks form and gently fold into the muffin batter.
6. Spoon batter into the prepared muffin tray, evening out the top with the back of a wet spoon. If you have pumpkin filling to fill it up: spoon batter ¾ full, add a tbsp pumpkin cream cheese and cover with a

thin layer batter. Sprinkle with almond streusel (if desired).

7. Covering with aluminum foil at 15, bake for 20 to 28 minutes until deep golden and once a toothpick inserted towards the side comes out clean. Keep an eye for them to avoid overcooking.

8. Before removing, let it cool in the pan for 15 minutes. Cool it thoroughly in a rack when frosting. Please take note that these are best enjoyed when cold, once the flavors have had a chance to mingle.

9. Keep it airtight covered and refrigerated for up to 3 days.

For the Pumpkin Filling (optional):
1. In a medium bowl add pumpkin puree and cream cheese. Use an electric mixer to combine thoroughly. Add in vanilla extract, sweetener, and pumpkin pie spice until thoroughly combined. Cover and refrigerate until needed.

2. On the other hand, fill an ice cube tray and place it on the freezer until solid. It will be easier to set the filling onto the muffins, and they will retain their shape best. Though note that as the stuffing will expand when baked and collapse when cooling, the muffins will inevitably collapse somewhat.

For the Almond Streusel (optional)
1. Add coconut flour, almond flour, pumpkin pie spice, Pour to a food processor, add salt mix well. Add in butter and mix again until the mixture resembles

breadcrumbs. Add in pecans and blend until roughly chopped and combined.
2. Cover tightly and refrigerate until needed, and up to 5 days.

Chapter 6: Do's and Don'ts on Keto Thanksgiving

Holidays are incredibly stressful especially if you have recently changed to a new way of eating, especially if you are going home for the holidays and are going to be around people who don't eat the same kinds of foods you eat. This article can explain how to manage the holiday season. How to eat and how to do it in the least stressful way possible so that you can both feel good at the end.

Here is some advice for you to have an idea of what to eat and not to eat during the holiday feast.

Eat Umami Gravy, Not Traditional Gravy

Ingredients:

½ oz porcini mushrooms (dried)
2 tbsp ghee
2 onions (diced)
1 tsp tomato paste
½ tsp fish sauce
½ pound cremini mushrooms (sliced)
3 garlic cloves (minced)
4 cups bone broth
3 fresh thyme sprigs
kosher salt
black pepper (ground)

Procedure:

1. Rinse the dried mushrooms with cold water. Place them in a small bowl. Pour enough water to cover the mushrooms. To soften, set aside for at least 30 minutes.
2. Melt the ghee over medium heat in a medium saucepan. Add onions and sauté for 10 to 15 minutes or until translucent.
3. Put the tomato paste and fish sauce.
4. Stir to distribute the umami boosters evenly.
5. Cook mushrooms for about 10 minutes until the liquid is released and evaporated before dumping in the sliced mushrooms.

6. Remove the reconstituted porcini mushrooms out of the bowl of water, and roughly chop them up.
7. In a saucepan, cook the garlic for 30 seconds or until fragrant.
8. Mix in the reformed dried mushrooms, pour in the broth and add in the thyme sprigs.
9. Lower heat to medium-low to maintain a steady low boil. Cook for about 30 minutes until the gravy has reduced by half. Wait patiently—you want half of the liquid to evaporate to concentrate the flavors. Plus, you don't want the gravy to be thin and watery once blended.
10. Remove from the heat. Take out the thyme twigs and season to taste with salt and pepper.
11. Put the gravy into a blender and mix until smooth.

Eat Sugar Free Cranberry Blueberry Sauce, Not Super Sweet Cranberry Sauce

Ingredients:

12 oz cranberries (fresh or frozen)
1 cup water
⅓ cup pyure all purpose
2 cups blueberries (fresh or frozen)
¾ tsp cinnamon (ground)
¼ tsp nutmeg (ground)
⅛ tsp allspice (ground)

Procedure:

1. Wash cranberries and discard any bad ones.
2. Pour the cranberries in a medium saucepan with water and sweetener. Bring to a boil over high heat.
3. Lower heat to medium. Mix and simmer cranberries for 10 minutes or until the berries burst. Mash the cranberries slightly with a spoon. Remove from heat.
4. Stir in the blueberries, nutmeg, cinnamon, and allspice. Stir to combine.
5. Transfer to a bowl, cool slightly and place plastic wrap directly on top of sauce to cover. Refrigerate until chilled.

Eat Garlicky Mashed Cauliflower, Not Mashed Potatoes

Ingredients:

1-2 heads fresh cauliflower (roughly chopped into uniform, large pieces)
4 tbsp butter
2 tbsp cream cheese or sour cream (optional)
2 tbsp or more parmesan, grated (optional)
garlic powder, salt, pepper, and other spices to taste

Procedure:

1. In a large pot, bring a couple of quarts of water to a boil.
2. Add cauliflower and cook until tender.
3. Drain well.
4. Transfer cooked cauliflower to a large bowl. Add butter and if desired cream cheese or sour cream and Parmesan.
5. Use an hand mixer or immersion blender to blend until smooth and creamy.
6. Sprinkle with extra cheese(optional) and serve warm.
7. Top with freshly chopped parsley or chives for a nice garnish!

Eat Cauliflower Stuffing, Not Bread Stuffing

Ingredients:

2 medium heads of cauliflower
1 tsp olive oil
1 large yellow onion (diced)
1 garlic clove (minced)
4 stalks of celery (sliced thinly)
3 cups of mushrooms (sliced)
½ cup pecans (roughly chopped)
2 ½ tsp dried sage
1 T poultry seasoning
1 tsp red wine vinegar
1 tsp sea salt
¼ tsp black pepper

Procedure:

1. In a food processor, blend cauliflower until it reaches "rice" consistency.
2. Add olive oil to a large pan over medium-high heat.
3. Add garlic, onions, and celery and sauté for 5 mins.
4. Add in cauliflower. Cook for 10 minutes or until fully cooked.
5. Add mushrooms and continue cooking until they've begun to sweat (about another 5 mins)
6. Top with pecans, spices, and vinegar and cook for 1 min.
7. Serve warm or store in a refrigerator for up to 5 days.

Eat Brussels Sprouts Gratin, Instead of Green Bean Casserole

Ingredients:

2 tbsps olive oil
1 large shallot (minced)
2 cloves garlic (minced)
½ brussels sprouts (pound finely shredded
1 c kettle & fire mushroom chicken bone broth
1 c organic heavy cream
1 c organic mozzarella cheese (shredded)
kosher salt
1 pinch nutmeg
¼ c pine nuts (finely chopped)
4 sprigs thyme leaves (finely chopped)
2 tbsps parmesan cheese (grated)

Procedure:

1. Pour the olive oil in a large saucepan over medium heat. Add garlic and shallots and cook, stir until soft for 2 to 3 minutes.
2. Put Brussels sprouts and stir to combine.
3. Pour bone broth to the pot and stir to combine. Cook for about 3 to 5 minutes until the Brussels sprouts are just soft. Mix in the heavy cream and cheese. Add the nutmeg and a couple of generous

pinches of salt. Cook until cheese is completely melted, 1 to 2 minutes.
4. In the meantime, combine the pine nuts, thyme, and parmesan cheese in a small bowl. Add a bit of salt and toss gently to combine.
5. Gently divide the Brussels sprouts and cream mixture evenly between the four ramekins and top with the pine nut mixture.
6. Put the bowls on a sheet pan. Transfer to the oven. Cook for about 10-12 minutes until the gratin is bubbly and the pine nut crust is golden brown. Remove from the oven, let it sit and serve.

Eat Almond Flour Pumpkin Pie, Never a Traditional Pumpkin Pie

Ingredients:

Crust:
2 ½ c almond flour
⅓ c erythritol
¼ tsp sea salt
¼ cup ghee (measured solid, then melted)
1 large egg
½ tsp vanilla extract (optional)

Pie:
1 15-oz can pumpkin (blended)
½ cup heavy cream
2 large egg (at room temperature)
⅔ cup powdered erythritol
2 tsp pumpkin pie spice
¼ tsp sea salt
1 tsp vanilla extract (optional)
1 tsp blackstrap molasses (optional)

Procedure:

Crust:
1. Preheat the oven to 350 °F. Align the bottom of a 9 inches round pie pan with parchment paper, or grease well.

2. Mix the almond flour, erythritol, and sea salt in a large bowl.
3. Beat the egg and melted ghee, until mix well. (If using vanilla, mix with the melted ghee before adding to the dry ingredients.) The "dough" will be dry and crumbly. Keep stirring, mixing, and pressing, until there is no almond flour powder left and it's uniform. On the other hand, mix it using a food processor.
4. In the lower part of the prepared pan press the dough. You can flute the edges of desire; if it crumbles when doing this, just press it back together. Poke holes carefully in the surface using a fork to prevent bubbling.
5. Bake for 10-12 minutes, until lightly golden. (Add fillings only after pre-baking.)

Pie:
1. Make the sweet almond flour pie crust by following the directions above.
2. In the meantime, beat together all remaining ingredients at medium-low speed, until smooth. (Remember: don't overmix.)
3. When done baking the pie crust, reduce the oven temperature to 325 °F. Let it cool for 10 minutes or longer if you have time.
4. Pour the filling into the crust. Gently press on the counter to release air bubbles.
5. Bake until the pie is almost set but still slightly jiggly in the center for 40-50 minutes. (Check it once in a

while, and if you see the crust starts to brown, cover the edge of the crust with foil and return to the oven until done with the filling. It should still wiggle a bit in the center, like a custard before it sets.) Cool completely on the counter, then refrigerate at least 1 hour before slicing. Pie can be refrigerated overnight.

Tips to stay in Keto Diet during Thanksgiving

1. Avoid foods that are high in carbs. Do not stress yourself when you end up eating forbidden foods- just compensate during other meals. It is better to have a handful list of foods to keep you on track.
2. If you are going to someone's place for Thanksgiving lunch or dinner, bring at least two dishes that you can eat. Give them also heads up about your diet.
3. If bringing food isn't an option, eat something before you go so you won't be hungry when you get there.
4. Before meals, drink lemon water or apple cider vinegar to improve digestion and absorption of the nutrients you're eating.
5. Always have a positive mindset towards foods.

Chapter 7: Keto Thanksgiving Turkey Recipes

Keto Thanksgiving Turkey

Ingredients:

14-16 lbs whole turkey thawed (6.57kg)
1 large onion
½ lemon
5 sticks celery
4 cloves garlic
3 tbsp olive oil
1 tbsp salt
1 tbsp black pepper
herb butter
½ cup salted butter
¼ parsley (chopped)
4 cloves garlic
1 tbsp rosemary

Procedure:

1. For the butter, mince the garlic. Combine the ingredients in a small bowl.
2. Preheat the oven to 170C/325F.
3. Wash the turkey thoroughly. Dry the skin and place in a roasting rack inside a large roasting pan.
4. Chop the onion and celery. Slice the lemon into wedges. Mince the garlic.
5. Fill the turkey's stomach with the veggies from step 4.
6. Put your hands between the skin and the breast meat working down the leg to loosen the covering

of the bird. Take some of your butter mixtures and rub it all over the skin, the breast, and leg meat. Coat as much as you can.

7. Spill out the olive oil all over the turkey and sprinkle the salt and pepper all over. Bond the legs of the turkey together with kitchen twine or ovenproof string.

8. On the middle rack of the oven place the turkey breast side up and bake for 2.5 hours to 3 hours. Halfway through, saturate the turkey juice all over the skin. At 2.5 hours, check the thermometer. It should register at 160F. If a probe thermometer is not available use handheld thermometer, open the oven and check, If it doesn't reach the required temperature, cook it a bit longer for about 10-40 mins.

9. Take the breast meat out of the oven once it registers at 160 F. Cover the dish with aluminum foil for 30 minutes.

10. After that, you can start carving it.

Dry-Brined Orange Rosemary Roasted Turkey

Ingredients:

1 10-12 lbs diestel organic young turkey
2 tbsp kosher salt
2 tbsp extra virgin olive oil
1 tbsp rosemary (chopped fresh), plus two large sprigs (divided)
2 tbsp orange juice (fresh)
1 tbsp orange zest
1 tsp smoked paprika
½ tsp black pepper (freshly ground)
1 small onion (peeled and quartered)
1 small navel orange (cut)
4 small cloves garlic (smashed and peeled)
kitchen twine (for trussing)

Procedure:

1. 3 days before cooking, pat the turkey dry with paper towels and place on a rimmed baking sheet. Sprinkle evenly with the kosher salt on the outside and inside the cavity and refrigerate uncovered until 2 hours before ready to cook.
2. Once the turkey is out of the refrigerator and let it stand for 2 hours at room temperature.
3. Preheat the oven to 350 degrees.
4. Place the olive oil, chopped rosemary, orange juice, zest, smoked paprika, and black pepper in a small

bowl and whisk until combined. Coat the skin of the turkey with the olive oil mixture evenly.

5. Place the onion, orange, garlic cloves, and remaining two sprigs of rosemary inside the cavity of the turkey. Truss the turkey legs using the kitchen twine, and tuck the wing tips underneath the turkey.

6. Place the turkey in the oven and cook for 2 - 2½ hours.

7. Let the turkey stand for 20 minutes covered loosely with foil, then place on a cutting board. Carve and enjoy!

Garlic Herb Bacon Wrapped Turkey Breast

Ingredients:

3 tbsp balsamic vinegar
2 tbsp olive oil
6 sprigs fresh rosemary (divided)
6 sprigs fresh thyme (divided)
2 tbsp steak seasoning
6 cloves garlic (crushed)
3-4 lb boneless turkey breast
10 slices bacon

Procedure:

1. Preheat the oven to 400°F.
2. Whisk the balsamic vinegar & olive oil together in a small bowl. Chop 4 sprigs of rosemary & 4 sprigs of thyme, add to the pan with the steak seasoning & crushed garlic.
3. Brush this mixture over the turkey breast.
4. Place the two remaining sprigs of rosemary & thyme on top of the turkey.
5. Weave the bacon slices together over the turkey.
6. Tuck the bacon under the turkey. For the easy removal after the turkey has baked, make sure the ends of the rosemary and thyme sprigs slightly stick out at the end.
7. Place the bacon wrapped turkey on top of a wire rack on a foil-lined baking sheet.
8. Brush any extra herb rub on top of the bacon.

9. Put the turkey in the oven and bake for an hour.
10. Remove the sprigs of rosemary & thyme from under the bacon and slice the turkey.
11. Serve and enjoy the salty, garlic, herb, crispy, bacon goodness!

Herbed Mayonnaise Roast Turkey

Ingredients:

1 10 lbs fresh turkey (if using frozen make sure it's thawed)
1 cup mayonnaise
2 tbsp orange zest
1 tbsp fresh rosemary (minced)
1 tbsp fresh thyme (minced)
1 tbsp fresh sage (minced)
1 tbsp orange juice
kosher salt and pepper to taste
2 oranges (cut into wedges)

Procedure:

1. Preheat oven to 400 degrees.
2. Remove innards from the inside of the turkey and add turkey to your roasting pan.
3. Dry off the turkey skin using a paper towel lightly dry off the turkey skin.
4. Mix mayonnaise, orange zest, rosemary, thyme, sage, and orange juice in a small bowl.
5. Spread mayonnaise mixture all over the turkey and inside the cavity. Use your hands for this job because it is the easiest way to coat the whole turkey.
6. Drizzle the turkey with kosher salt and pepper.
7. Stuff the stomach of the bird with orange wedges and any remaining fresh herbs you might have.

8. Put a pop-up timer into the meaty part of the breast. Press it down into the turkey until the timer is flush with the skin.
9. Place turkey into the oven. Cook for about 30 minutes at 400 degrees. Lower temperature to 350 degrees and cook until timer pops up or internal temperature is 180 degrees.
10. When your turkey gets too browned, merely tents it with foil for a bit then remove the foil to continue frying until fully cooked.
11. Let it rest for 30 minutes to 1 hour then carve and enjoy!

Roasted Garlic Turkey Breast

Ingredients:

1 large head of garlic (top cut off)
avocado oil (or other variety)
salt
black pepper
2 tbsp unsalted butter (softened at room temp)
2 ¾ – 3-pound turkey breast (bone-in and skin-on)
1 tsp italian seasoning
½ tsp paprika
1 tsp fresh thyme leaves

Procedure:

1. Preheat the oven to 400°.
2. Drizzle a little oil over the cut garlic, sprinkle some salt and pepper and wrap each tightly in a square of foil.
3. Roast for 45 minutes, until soft and golden-brown; allow to cool, and once the garlic can be touched, squeeze the roasted garlic from their papers; mush into a paste using a knife or fork, then reduce the oven temp to 375°.
4. Add the roasted garlic "paste" into a small dish, along with the softened butter, and blend the two thoroughly, along with a pinch of salt and pepper, as well.
5. Place your turkey breast on a work surface, tenderly place your fingers between the flesh and the skin,

slightly pulling it apart. Add the garlic-butter under the skin, over the meat, spread it evenly. Reserve about one tsp. of the garlic butter, and rub it over the surface, as well.

6. Next, to a small bowl add ½ tsp. of salt, ½ tsp. of black pepper, Italian seasoning and the paprika, and combine this seasoning mixture; spread it all over the skin of the turkey.

7. Put a digital thermometer to the thickest part of the breast, and then place the breast onto a baking sheet with foil, and roast it for about an hour and 15-20 minutes, or until the thermometer registers 165°.

8. Allow the turkey breast to rest for about 10 minutes before slicing the meat; sprinkle over the thyme, and serve.

Keto Turkey with Cream-Cheese Sauce

Ingredients:

2 tbsp butter
20 oz turkey (breast part)
2 cups of heavy whipping cream
7 oz cream cheese
salt and pepper
1/3 cup small capers
1 tbsp tamari soy sauce

Procedure:

1. Preheat the oven to 350°F.
2. Melt the first half of the butter over medium heat in a large ovenproof pan. Season the turkey generously and fry until brown.
3. Finish the turkey breasts in the oven. When the turkey is already cooked and has an internal temperature of at least 165°F, place it on a plate.
4. In a small saucepan, pour turkey drippings. Add cream cheese and heavy cream. Stir and let it boil. Reduce the heat. Let it simmer until thickened. Add salt and pepper to taste. Use Japanese gluten-free tamari to add more color and flavor.
5. Melt remaining butter in a medium frying pan over high heat. Quickly sauté the capers until crispy.
6. Serve and enjoy the turkey with sauce and fried capers.

Porcini Mushroom Crusted Roasted Turkey Breast

Ingredients:

1 turkey breast (approximately 8 lbs.)
1 cup porcini mushrooms (dried)
1 tsp bell's turkey seasoning
1 tbsp kosher salt
½ tsp ground black pepper
¼ cup butter (softened)
¼ cup mayonnaise

For the pan gravy:
⅓ cup sour cream

Procedure:

1. In a blender grind the Porcini mushrooms into dust. Add seasoning, salt, and pepper and mix well.
2. Whip together the butter and mayonnaise until smooth. Add the seasoning mix, mushroom powder and stir until well incorporated.
3. Take out the turkey from the packaging and remove any innards from the cavity. Rinse and pat dry.
4. Put the turkey in a large pan. Remove the skin from the meat by sliding your hand underneath the skin be careful not to break it.

5. Stuff the mushroom mixture liberally under the skin, and massage the outside of the skin, to distribute it evenly.
6. Spread the remaining butter mixture on the outside of the skin and make sure the skin is covering the meat and hasn't pulled away from the top.
7. Drizzle with additional salt and pepper if desired.
8. Roast the turkey upright in a 400°F oven for an hour and 15 minutes.
9. To prevent meat from drying out when cutting, let the turkey rest for one hour before carving.

Procedure for the gravy:
1. After carving pour off pan juices and remove most of the fat that floats to the top.
2. Pour ⅓ cup of sour cream into the defatted pan juices. Season with salt and pepper to taste before serving.

Keto Pickle Juice Brine Turkey Recipe

Ingredients:

1 large container of pickles
bag of ice
reynolds oven bags (turkey size)
1 tbsp black peppercorn or black pepper
2 sprigs of fresh thyme
2 sprigs of fresh rosemary
3 bay leaves
4 – 6 cloves of garlic
3 cups of water
2 teaspoons kosher salt
Optional: 1 tablespoon McCormick's Grill Mates Montreal Steak seasoning or any of your other favorite seasonings that work well with Turkey

Procedure:

1. To get the oils from the leaves, peel the rosemary off of the steam and dice a few of them.
2. Defrost the turkey and place it into a large poultry bag or cooler.
3. Pour all the ingredients (seasonings, pickles, water, and juice) on top of the bird in the cooler. Make sure that the liquid covers most of the turkey. Add some more water if you don't have enough pickle juice to cover it.
4. Put the poultry bag with turkey in the refrigerator. If you don't have enough space put it on a cooler, add

a bag of ice on the top of the turkey to allow it to stay cool for the next 12 hours. Marinate the turkey for more than 12 hours but no more than 24 hours ahead of time.

5. The refrigerating hours depends on the pound of the meat. In every pound, you have 1 hour to refrigerate it. So, if you have a 12 lb turkey, you need to refrigerate this for 12 hours. Add ice to the cooler as needed.

6. Remove the turkey from the brine marinade. Discard the brine marinade.

7. Place the turkey into the turkey steam bag and place about two more cups of water in the bag so it can create steam when it's cooking.

Roasted Turkey w/ Sage Butter

Ingredients:

turkey (12 – 14 lb)
½ cup butter (1 stick, softened)
2 tbsp fresh sage (minced)
2 tbsp fresh garlic (minced)
1 tbsp kosher salt
1 tsp freshly ground pepper
1 lemon (quartered)
2 small apples (quartered)

Procedure:

1. Preheat your oven to 400 F and adjust your racks to fit the turkey into it.
2. Remove the neck and innards from the turkey and rinse the bird inside and out. Pat dry.
3. Combine the ingredients, the softened butter, sage, garlic, salt, and butter in a small bowl. From the back of the bird, glide your fingers all over the skin. Spread the remaining butter over the rest of the skin of the turkey.
4. Fill the cavity of the bird with quartered lemons and apples. Put the remaining fruits into your roasting pan.
5. In the roasting pan place the bird upside down – this will avoid the breast from drying out. Roast at 400 degrees for 1 hour. Remove it from the oven and turn over nicely. Roast the other side for another 1

hour. Using a meat thermometer test the thickest part of the thigh for 165 degrees. If it does not meet the required temperature, test it again after 15 minutes. Take it out from the oven and let it rest for one hour.

6. Put the pan juices into a measuring cup, while the turkey is resting. Separate 90% of the fat and then add ½ cup of water and ½ tsp of xanthan gum to thicken it. Process in a blender and reheat just before serving.

Instant Pot Turkey Breast with Gravy

Ingredients:

6.5 lb. turkey (breast part)
paprika, onion powder, garlic powder, salt, and pepper
to taste
1 can turkey or chicken broth
1 large onion (quartered)
1 stock celery (cut in large pieces)
1 sprig of thyme
3 cloves of garlic
3 tbsp cornstarch
3 tbsp cold water

Procedure:

1. Season turkey breast liberally with spices.
2. Stuff with onion, celery, garlic, and thyme.
3. Saute the turkey breast with a bit of butter until brown. Leave turkey breast side up when done
4. Add chicken broth.
5. Lock lid in place, set 30 minutes cooking time and select High Pressure.
6. Turn off pressure cooker when it whistles. Use a natural pressure release for about 10 minutes, after that do a quick pressure release to release any remaining pressure.
7. Carefully remove the lid when valves drop. Check if the turkey is done using an instant-read

thermometer. It should be 165°. If it isn't 165°, lock the lid in place and cook it for a few more minutes.

8. Remove the turkey and put it on a large plate when it has reached 165 degrees. Cover with foil and place under a broiler to brown the turkey breast.

9. Strain and skim the fat off the broth if desired.

10. Whisk together cornstarch, cold water, and the broth in cooking pot.

11. Select Sauté and stir until broth thickens. Add salt and pepper to taste.

12. Remove breast from broiler and sliced the turkey and serve immediately.

Chapter 8: Keto Comforting Soups for Thanksgiving

Roasted Tomato and Red Pepper Soup

Ingredients:

Version 1
890 g tomatoes (quartered)
200 g red bell pepper (cut into large pieces and seeds removed)
50 g onion (cut)
30 g lemon juice (fresh)
⅓ cup olive oil
1 tsp salt
1 tsp dried oregano
1 tsp sweet paprika
¼ oz peeled garlic cloves
1 qt vegetable broth/chicken broth
¼ cup rough basil leaves (chopped, fresh)

Version 2
890 g tomatoes (quartered)
200 g red bell pepper (cut into large pieces and seeds removed)
50 g cut onion
30 g lemon juice (fresh)
⅓ cup olive oil
1 tsp salt
1 tsp dried oregano
1 tsp sweet paprika
¼ oz garlic cloves (peeled)
1 qt vegetable broth/chicken broth
¼ cup rough basil leaves (chopped fresh)

⅛ tsp. cayenne pepper
2 tsp garam masala
1 tsp turmeric powder
1 can coconut cream

Procedure:

Preheat the oven at 400 F. Place a baking sheet with parchment paper

VERSION 1

1. Cut the tomatoes into eight parts, the bell pepper/capsicum into large pieces, onions into large wedges, and separate the layers of an onion, peel the whole garlic cloves, remove fresh basil leaves from the stem. Put into a big bowl
2. Add salt, dry oregano, and sweet paprika into cut vegetables. Mix to distribute the spices evenly.
3. Pour the oil and lemon juice over the vegetables.
4. Distribute the vegetables evenly into the parchment lined the baking sheet
5. Place it in the middle part of your preheated oven and bake for 20 minutes.
6. Five minutes before the vegetables done, pour your stock into a medium soup pot and bring the broth to boil.
7. Put the roasted vegetables and basil into the simmering stock. Let it boil and cook for another 5 minutes.

8. Blend the stock and vegetables in small batches. Pour into a clean bowl.

VERSION 2
1. Put the pureed soup back into your cooking pot
2. Add 1 can of full-fat coconut cream
3. Add cayenne pepper, garam masala, turmeric, stir and simmer for 5 minutes
4. To serve. Sprinkle with 1 tbsp. cream over the soup and glaze with a few small fresh basil leaves. Enjoy!

Creamy Cheddar Cheese and Broccoli Soup

Ingredients:

Cheddar and Broccoli Soup:
1 tbsp unsalted butter
¼ of a medium onion (grated)
¼ cup unsalted butter (melted)
1 tsp xanthan gum
2 cups heavy cream
2 cups chicken stock
¼ cup sour cream
1 ½ cup broccoli florets (bite size)
1 cup sharp cheddar cheese (grated)
¼ cup bacon pieces
½ tsp salt
¼ tsp black pepper
¼ tsp ground nutmeg

Procedure:

1. Cut broccoli into bite-sized pieces. Prepare about a cup and a half.
2. Grate a quarter part of medium onion and set aside.
3. In a pot on medium high heat, add 1 tbsp of unsalted butter; grated onion and cook for about a minute or two.
4. Add ¼ cup of melted butter and 1 tsp. Xanthan gum. Mix and cook for about 3 to 4 minutes.
5. Add 2 cups of chicken stock; 2 cups of heavy cream; and a little of sour cream.

6. Add some salt; ground black pepper; and finish with a touch of ground nutmeg.
7. Stir to combine and let cook until it boils. Decrease the heat to medium then add the broccoli.
8. Cook the broccoli until it reaches your desired texture of it. Add ¼ cup of bacon pieces. Stir to mix. Pour 1 cup of shredded sharp cheddar cheese.
9. Whisk until all the cheese melted. You'll see a change to a nice golden color. Pour into a bowl; garnish with some cheese; and a little bacon; and enjoy!

Chicken Cordon Bleu Soup

Ingredients:

16 oz cooked chicken (shredded)
16 oz ham (diced)
2 tbsp unsalted butter
8 oz cream cheese
1 cup heavy cream
4 cups chicken stock
8 oz swiss cheese (shredded)
1 tsp salt
2 tsp poultry seasoning
½ tsp ground black pepper
¼ tsp cayenne pepper
dried chives as garnish

Procedure:

1. To a stock pot on medium high heat, add two tablespoons of unsalted butter.
2. Add the diced ham and stir and cook until it starts to brown a bit. It should take 3 to 5 minutes.
3. Add some heavy cream and give a stir.
4. Add 8 ounces of softened cream cheese. Wait until the cream cheese fully melted.
5. Add the chicken and mix to incorporate. Pour in four cups of chicken stock give that a mix to blend.
6. Season the soup with some poultry seasoning; salt; ground black pepper; and just a bit of cayenne. Mix until well combined.

7. Bring the soup to boil and cook for about 15 minutes to allow all the flavors to come together. After it's cooked a bit, give a taste and adjust for seasoning.

8. Now add the shredded Swiss cheese - half at a time. Adding the cheese this way will provide us with a smoother texture.

9. Once the cheese fully melted, give a final stir and serve warm. Garnish with little extra cheese, some dry chives and enjoy!

Cream of Mushroom Soup

Ingredients:

12 oz butter

1 ¾ lb white button mushrooms (sliced)

3 ½ oz oyster mushrooms (optional - for extra flavor)

3 ½ oz portobello mushrooms (sliced)

3 ½ oz onions (chopped)

3 ½ oz heavy whipping cream

2 qt chicken broth

2 tbsp dry red wine or red wine vinegar

2 tsp salt

1 tsp pepper

2 tsp garlic powder/1 tbsp fresh grated garlic

2 tbsp fresh thyme (branches)

Procedure:

1. Place the pot over medium-high heat. Add about 2 tbsp of butter and melt it.
2. Pour the sliced mushrooms and set heat to high. Stir and mix the mushrooms until cook and brown. Remove from heat and set aside some nicely-shaped mushrooms, which can use as a garnish for the soup.
3. In a separate pot, add the remaining butter. Melt and then add the chopped onions. Saute until the onions are transparent. Add the onions and all the butter to the browned mushrooms.
4. Pour dry red wine or red wine vinegar and mix.

5. Cook for a few minutes while stirring.
6. Pour the chicken stock and the sprigs of thyme and bring to a light simmer.
7. Cook for about ten mins.
8. Add the cream. Continue cooking at a light boil for five more minutes
9. Use a fork to fish out the sprigs of thyme. Discard the thyme
10. Add a bit of salt and pepper to taste and stir well.
11. Spoon out the soup content and puree in small batches.
12. Blend while the soup is still hot. Puree until all the mushrooms processed well, and you have a smooth texture. Pour into a tureen or clean bowl
13. Garnish with the reserved mushrooms. Enjoy!

Zucchini and Basil Low Carb Keto Soup

Ingredients:

450g (1lb) zucchini
2 cloves of garlic
2 cup (470ml) of chicken broth
1 tbsp olive oil
½ tsp salt
½ tsp pepper
⅓ cup of basil
½ cup of heavy cream

Procedure:

1. Cut Zucchini into chunks
2. Add olive oil to a pot
3. Fry the chopped garlic in olive oil until it turns lightly gold
4. Add zucchini, salt, and pepper into the pan and cook until soft, for about 5 minutes
5. Mix the chicken broth in, bring it to a boil and simmer for about 10 minutes
6. Puree the soup until smooth, and put it back to the pot
7. Mix in heavy cream
8. Serve hot or cold.

Chapter 9: Keto Diet Desserts Made Easy

Holiday Season is coming. Most of us are looking forward to this season every year. All are preparing, especially when it comes to things like food, considering that you are on a diet. Number one on our list is getting the dessert right. If you can get the dessert right, everything else will fall into place.

We will provide you with dessert recipes that you'll surely love. You can enjoy thanksgiving desserts without affecting your Keto Diet. It's something that you can all share. Nobody wants to feel left out when it comes to sweets. This desserts recipes are made easy, so you don't have to worry about creating multiple desserts.

Top 10 Keto Diet Desserts For Thanksgiving:

1. Chocolate Cheesecake Keto Brownies

Ingredients:

100 g unsalted butter
100 g 90% dark chocolate
2 eggs
¼ cup stevia
1 tsp vanilla essence
pinch of salt
¼ cup coconut flour
200 g cream cheese (chopped into bite-sized pieces)

Procedure:

1. Preheat the oven to 350 F and grease an oven proof dish.
2. Melt together the butter and chocolate over low heat.
3. When the butter and chocolate melt, set aside to cool.
4. Mix together the eggs, stevia, vanilla, and salt in a large bowl.
5. When smooth combine with the chocolate until well mix.

6. Gently stir through the coconut flour, 1 tbsp at a time.
7. Prepare oven dish and place half of the brownie batter on it.
8. Sprinkle with the chopped cream cheese and lastly spread over the other half of the brownie batter.
9. Put into the oven for 20 minutes or until cooked.
10. Remove from the oven, cool and serve.

2. Low Carb Strawberry Cheesecake

Ingredients:

Crust:
¾ cup pecans
¾ cup almond flour
4 tbsp butter
2 tbsp splenda

Filling:
1½ lbs cream cheese
4 eggs
½ tbsp liquid vanilla
½ tbsp lemon juice
1 cup splenda
¼ cup sour cream
9 strawberries

Procedure:

1. Preheat the oven to 400 degrees
2. Crush the pecans
3. Melt 4 tbsp. butter, add pecans, Splenda and almond flour in a small saucepan.
4. Mix the crust in the pot for several minutes until combined
5. Grease a 9 inches springform pan and line the bottom with the crust
6. Cook for 7 minutes at 400 degrees until it just starts to brown

7. For the filling, combine all the ingredients at a room temperature in a stand mixer and mix well
8. Slice strawberries and align it on the side of the crust (optional)
9. On top of the crust/strawberries add filling.
10. Optionally top the cheesecake with strawberries
11.
12. Place the cheesecake in the oven at 400 degrees, once it's inside, lower the temperature at 250 degrees.
13. Cook for about 60-90 minutes or until the cheesecake has set.
14. Let it cool, and then place in the refrigerator, serve cold with whip cream

3. Keto Sugar-Free Chocolate Mousse

Ingredients:

50 g dark chocolate 85%
15 g salted butter
1 tbsp cocoa powder
200 ml whipping cream
stevia to taste

Procedure:

1. In the microwave melt butter and chocolate for about 30 minutes and mix.
2. Whip together cream, cocoa powder, and stevia
3. Add in the chocolate and butter mix
4. Stir till soft peaks are formed and put into bowls.
5. Refrigerate for 1 hour at least and serve cold.

4. Almond Butter Cookies

Ingredients

1 cup almond butter
1 egg
⅓ – ½ cup erythritol to taste
¼ tsp salt
2 tbsp cacao nibs

Procedure:

1. Preheat oven to 350°F.
2. Combine the almond butter, egg, salt, and erythritol in a bowl. Whip with a hand mixer until a creamy, well-combined mixture forms.
3. Stir in your cacao nibs.
4. Use a small cookie scoop and spoon balls of dough about 2 teaspoons in size onto a sprayed baking sheet lined with parchment.
5. Flattened the dough by pressing your it down on the tops.
6. Bake for about 15-17 minutes, until brown. Cookies will be thick as they cool.
7. Allow cooling slightly before devouring!

5. Keto Fat Bombs

Ingredients:

3 oz coconut oil
1.5 oz cream cheese
1.5 ounces torani sugar-free vanilla
1.5 tsp unsweetened cocoa powder
3 oz chocolate
12 drops ez-sweetz
sunflower butter

Procedure:

1. Combine all the items except the Sunflower butter and microwave for 30 seconds.
2. Mix the ingredients, if the chocolate is not fully melted, microwave again and continue stirring.
3. In the mold you are using, pour a base layer.
4. Use a spoon and place a dollop of Sunflower Butter in the center.
5. Fill all the chocolate mold to the top.
6. Place on the refrigerator until the chocolate hardens, when hard push them out of the mold.
7. Store in the fridge.

6. Keto Caramel Sauce and Soft Caramel Fat Bomb

Ingredients:

3 ½ tbsp unsalted butter
6 tbsp lakanto golden monk fruit sweetener
7 tbsp heavy whipping cream
⅛ tsp salt
1 tsp pure vanilla extract
¼ cup water

Procedure:

1. In a small pot make a simple syrup by adding the water and sweetener. Bring to boil, stirring continuously, and cook over medium heat until the sweetener is dissolved entirely and a deep golden color.
2. Add the butter in a deep sided frying pan and cook over medium heat until the butter solids separate and turn a golden brown.
3. Add the salt and the vanilla and mix.
4. Add the simple syrup to the pan, and stir well. Cook for a minute or two to combine and for the color to deepen to a golden brown.
5. Add the cream, stirring and being careful (CAUTION: the addition of cream will cause frothing and bubbling which is extremely hot).

6. Cook over medium-low heat at a light simmer for about 15 to 20 minutes, continuously stir it so that the caramel does not burn.
7. Let it cool and store in an airtight glass container or pour into molds for fat bombs.

7. Keto Chia Pudding

Ingredients:

2 tbsp chia seeds
heavy cream
coconut milk
vanilla
other atkins friendly ingredients

Procedure:

1. Place 2 tbsp of Chia Seeds into a bowl, glass or jar.
2. Top with half a cup of liquid, from any or a combination of the following: Low Carb Yoghurt, Cream, Almond Milk or your milk of choice, Coconut Milk.
3. Combine the liquid into the chia seeds until completely incorporated.
4. You can enjoy your chia pudding straight away, or refrigerate to thicken.
5. You can add Toppings. (Optional)

8. Low Carb Lemon Mousse Recipe

Ingredients:

½ cup mascarpone cheese
1 lemon
2 tablespoons stevia
1 cup cream

Procedure:

1. Whisk the mascarpone in a bowl until smooth.
2. Grate the peeling of the lemon over the mascarpone then cut in half and squeeze the juice over.
3. Add the stevia and whisk until smooth.
4. Mix the cream in a separate bowl until thick.
5. Fold the thickened cream into the lemon mixture.
6. Add some sweetener to taste and then move into a serving bowl.
7. Refrigerate for a few hours to thicken. Serve and enjoy.

9. Sweet and Creamy Lemon Lime Bites

Ingredients:

Crust ingredients:
½ cup almond flour
1 cup ground pecans
¼ cup coconut oil (melted)
liquid sugar
1 tsp nutmeg

½ tsp almond extract
½ tsp salt

Filling ingredients:
16 oz cream cheese
¼ cup sour cream
2 eggs
1 tbsp vanilla
⅔ cup sugar
1 lime (juice and zest)
1 lemon (juice and zest)more lemon and lime zest for garnish (optional)

Procedure:

1. To a medium mixing bowl, add a half a cup of almond flour; 1 cup of ground pecans; a little ground nutmeg; and a bit of salt. Give that a mix to combine.
2. Now add a quarter cup of melted coconut oil and a liquid sugar substitute equal to two tablespoons of regular sugar.
3. With your hands, combine and mix to a mini muffin tin, line with small paper muffin cups.
4. Add the crust mixture to each cup. Use a small measuring spoon.
5. After filling each cup, with your fingers, gently press the crust down to compact. Preheat the oven at 350°F for 10 minutes and place the crust in the center.

6. For the filling, add zest and juice from one lemon and one lime. Taste each, be sure only to get the top layer. After zesting, extract the juice from each and set aside.

7. To a large mixing bowl, add 16 ounces of softened cream cheese; two lightly beaten eggs; a granulated sugar substitute equal to ⅔ cups of regular sugar; ¼ cup of sour cream; and our lemon and lime juice.

8. With an electric mixer, beat until all the ingredients are combined.

9. Add some vanilla extract and the zests of our lemon and lime. Mix again to incorporate. Make sure to scrape down the sides during mixing.

10. For refrigerated crusts, add about a tablespoon or so of the filling into each cup. When filled, place in the middle of a preheated 350°F oven for about 17 minutes.

11. When done, remove and place on a cooling rack to cool. When they've reached room temperature, place in the refrigerator for at least three hours.

12. When thoroughly chilled, you'll enjoy a delicious, zesty bite-size little treat that has just a bit over one net carb. If you're serving these for a party, dress them up a bit by garnishing with a bit of lemon and lime zest before serving.

10. Chocolate Fondue

Ingredients:

1 ¼ cups heavy whipping cream

7 tbsp monk fruit sweetener
8 tbsp cocoa powder (dutch processed)
2 tbsp unsalted butter
2 tbsp coconut oil
2 tsp pure vanilla extract
1 tsp instant unflavored coffee
¼ tsp) fine salt

Procedure:

1. In a stove place a small pot add about 1 to 2 inches of water. Bring to light boil, then reduce the heat to maintain a light simmer. Observe this before you place your bowl with the chocolate ingredients on top
2. Measure all the ingredients.Pour all the ingredients to a bowl that will fit over the pot with simmering water. On top of the pot with the boiling water place the bowl
3. Using a spatula or whisk, slowly and continuously stir until all the ingredients are melt and well mixed. If mixture is getting too hot, remove the bowl from the heat. Place on counter and continue stirring until everything is melt and you have a rich glossy mixture
4. Put the chocolate mixture into the fondue pot and serve

Optional

- You can add fresh fruit: strawberries, raspberries, blackberries, or other fruit with a low glycemic index and low carb load
- Cubes of Naked Vanilla Sponge Cake – it is recommended its firm texture and better consistency when dipped into the chocolate fondue. ENJOY!

No Bake Keto Thanksgiving Dessert:

Keto Cheesecake Recipe

Ingredients:

For the Crust:
10 g almond flour
10 g pecans (very finely chopped)
1 ½ tsp sweetener
quarter tsp of cinnamon
1 ½ tsp grass-fed butter (melted)

For the Filling:
40 g sour cream
70 g cream cheese
2 tbsp grass-fed butter
½ tsp vanilla extract
⅛ of a tsp of lemon juice
2 to 3 tbsp sweetener

Procedure:

For the Crust:

1. Put the 10 grams of my almond flour 10 grams of the finely chopped pecans on a pan.
2. Fry it up on a pan until golden brown the nuts are toasted and do not skip this step toasting the nuts it makes a tremendous difference in the way how the crust will taste.
3. Add the butter, ½ teaspoon of a sweetener, quarter teaspoon of cinnamon whisk it up good together until it's all nicely combined.
4. Add the crust mixture into four little containers.
5. Press the dough carefully into the bottom o all four containers filled up with crusts.
6. Place them in a freezer while, working on the filling

For the Filling:

1. Add 40 grams of the sour cream into a pod, 70 grams of the cream cheese, 28 grams of grass-fed butter, half of a teaspoon of vanilla extract, eighth of the teaspoon of lemon juice and 3 tbsp of your sweetener.
2. Use your hand as a mixer and mix it all well together for about three to four minutes.
3. Use a ziplock and cut a little opening so you can swirl the filling into the small containers.
4. Put them in a freezer for about 40 minutes and then garnish them with some fresh strawberries you can use any berries of your choice.

Pumpkin Pie Smoothie Recipe

Ingredients:

¼ c pumpkin purée (frozen)
½ c vanilla flavored almond milk (unsweetened)
½ c heavy cream
1 tsp ground cinnamon
1 tsp pumpkin pie extract
¼ tsp vanilla extract
¼ tsp ground nutmeg
¼ cup (12 tsp) regular sugar

Procedure:

1. Start with a can of pumpkin puree and freeze it in a silicone mold in quarter cup amounts.
2. Add a quarter cup of the frozen pumpkin puree; a half cup of heavy cream; a half cup of vanilla flavored unsweetened almond milk; a liquid sugar substitute equal to 12 teaspoons of regular sugar; add the pumpkin pie extract; a little vanilla extract; some ground cinnamon; and just a little ground nutmeg to mixer or regular blender.
3. Blend or Mix the ingredients until smooth. Blend it a little longer to become thicker.
4. Add some extra almond milk to thin when it gets too thick.

No Bake Key Lime Pie

Ingredients:

1 pack lime Jello (sugar-free)
½ c boiling water
1 8oz package of cream cheese softened (fat-free)
1 tbsp lime juice
½ a lime peel (grated)
2 c cool whip

Procedure:

1. In a small bowl add one pack of sugar-free lime Jell-O and a half cup of boiling water. Mix it up until all that powder has dissolved completely.
2. In a large bowl add eight ounces of cream cheese softened at room temperature. Beat it until it's nice and smooth.
3. Slowly add the mix gelatin while mixing the cream cheese.
4. Add 1 tbsp of lime juice.
5. Grate the peel of a lime and add it on the mixture.
6. Add 2 cups of cool whip and mix it well. Don't over mix it just merely make sure mixture are all incorporated, mix it until it has nice even consistent color throughout.
7. Take a 9-inch pie dish and lightly spray it with some cooking spray then take the filling and fill the entire pie dish. Spread it out nice and evenly until all filled up.

8. Set this in the refrigerator for at least three hours three to four hours.
9. Cut it into a beautiful piece and serve.

Keto Mug Cake

Ingredients:

3 tbsp cream cheese (1 for cake, 2 for the icing)
1 large egg
2 tbsp milk
3 tsp coconut flour
1 tbsp olive oil
¼ tsp baking powder
1 tsp cinnamon powder
2 tbsp sweetener of your choice

Procedure:

1. On a bowl, add one tablespoon of olive oil and two tablespoons of whole milk and an egg.
2. Put one tablespoon of cream cheese into a separate bowl, pop it into the microwave for about 15 to 20 seconds for its nice creamy texture and once it comes, add it on the ramekin with olive oil, milk, and egg.
3. Mix and then add a ¼ teaspoon of baking powder, one teaspoon cinnamon, 3 tbsp of coconut flour and 2 tablespoons of sweeteners.
4. Stir again. Make sure the ingredients are nicely incorporated and blended.

120

5. For the icing, put two tablespoons of cream cheese in another bowl. Then place it in the microwave to get it nice and soft.
6. Add ½ a tablespoon of xylitol. Mix in the xylitol until you get a nice creamy texture.
7. Going back to the mixture, put it in a mug and place the cup in the microwave for about 2 minutes.
8. Take the mug out of the microwave, turn it upside-down, give it a tap and it usually comes out.
9. Turn it another way round to have a nice flat surface to put the icing. Add the icing and xylitol mixture and spread that all over the top.
10. Lastly, add some cinnamon on top and serve.

Chocolate Avocado Pudding

Ingredients:

¼ c cocoa powder (unsweetened)
1 medium avocado
10 drops liquid stevia
½ tsp vanilla extract
1 tsp pink salt

Procedure:

1. Place the avocado in a mixing bowl after removing the pit from it.
2. Add the ingredients: cocoa powder, stevia, and vanilla extract and mix with a fork until pudding forms.

3. Top with pink sea salt. Enjoy.

Low Carb Peanut Butter Balls

Ingredients:

1 cup peanut butter
1 cup almond flour
¼ cup powdered erythritol/swerve confectioners
3 oz unsweetened bakers chocolate

Procedure:

1. Combine peanut butter, almond flour, and sweetener. Combine well.
2. Place peanut butter mixture into the freezer for an hour.
3. Melt bakers chocolate in the microwave or double broiler.
4. Roll frozen peanut butter mixture into balls.
5. Insert a toothpick into balls and coat in melted chocolate.
6. Place chocolate coated peanut butter balls into the fridge to harden. Store in the fridge.

Low Carb Mug Cake

Ingredients:

3 tbsp almond flour

2 tbsp erythritol
1 large egg
1.5 tbsp butter
1.5 tbsp sour cream
¼ tsp ground cinnamon (topping)
⅛ tsp pink salt
¼ tsp vanilla extract
¼ tsp baking powder

Procedure:

1. Combine the ingredients: almond flour, baking powder, salt, erythritol, vanilla, and melted butter well.
2. Add egg and combine well.
3. Add sour cream and mix well.
4. Pour into mug or ramekin and microwave for 90 seconds. Keep an eye on it for when it rises too high.
5. Tip: If it rises high (over the rim) open the microwave door, let it deflate before finishing out the 90 seconds.

Chapter 10: More Keto Thanksgiving Recipes

Maple Bacon Carrots

Ingredients:

12 medium carrots (peeled)
12 bacon (strips)
¼ maple syrup
black pepper (freshly cracked)

Procedure:

1. Preheat oven to 400°F. Wrap each carrot with one slice of bacon. In a large baking sheet place, bacon ends down. Brush the bacon wrapped with maple syrup and season with black pepper.
2. Bake for 10 minutes, take it out from the oven. Brush with remaining maple syrup. Bake again for 15 minutes more, or until carrots are tender and bacon is crisp. Serve and enjoy.

Keto Peanut Butter Squares

Ingredients:

cooking spray (for pan)

1 ½ c peanut butter (smooth unsweetened)
1 ¼ c coconut flour
¼ c keto friendly powdered sugar (such as swerve)
1 tsp pure vanilla extract
pinch kosher salt
2 c keto friendly chocolate chips
2 tbsp coconut oil
1 tbsp flaky sea salt (for garnish)

Procedure:

1. Prepare an 8x8 baking pan, line parchment paper on it and grease with cooking spray. Combine coconut flour, peanut butter, powdered sugar, vanilla, and salt in a medium bowl. Mix until smooth and pour into prepared baking pan, flatten the top using a spatula. Put it on the freezer for 30 minutes to firm up.
2. Combine chocolate chips and coconut oil in a medium microwave-safe bowl. Microwave, stirring every 30 seconds, until smooth and pourable. Pour chocolate over peanut butter layer and smooth.
3. Garnish with flaky sea salt and place in freezer to harden, 2 hours or up to overnight.
4. When ready to serve, remove peanut butter bars from baking dish and cut into squares.

Cauliflower Stuffing

Ingredients:

4 tbsp butter
1 onion (chopped)
2 large carrots (peeled and chopped)
2 celery stalks (thinly sliced)
1 small head cauliflower (chopped)
1 cup mushrooms (chopped)
kosher salt
black pepper (freshly ground)
¼ cup fresh parsley (chopped)
2 tbsp fresh rosemary (chopped)
1 tbsp fresh sage (chopped)
½ cup vegetable or chicken broth

Procedure:

1. In a stove over medium heat melt the butter in a large pot . Add carrot, onion, and celery. Sauté until soft for about 7-8 mins.
2. Add mushrooms and cauliflower. Sprinkle with salt and pepper. Cook for about 8-10 minutes until tender.
3. Add rosemary, parsley, and sage. Stir until combined. Pour vegetable broth and cover with a lid. Cover until totally tender, and liquid is absorbed 15 minutes.
4. Serve and enjoy.

Triple-Cheese Bacon Spinach Dip

Ingredients:

10 slices bacon

1 to 8 oz. block cream cheese (softened)

⅓ cup mayonnaise

⅓ cup sour cream

1 tsp garlic powder

1 tsp paprika

1 lb frozen chopped spinach (defrosted and squeezed of excess liquid)

1 cup parmesan (grated)

1 cup shredded mozzarella (divided)

1 baguette (sliced and toasted)

Procedure:

1. Preheat oven to 350°F. Cook the bacon for 8 minutes in a large nonstick pan over medium heat. until crispy. Dry on a paper towel-lined plate, then chop.
2. Stir together sour cream, mayonnaise, cream cheese, garlic powder, and paprika in a large bowl. Season with salt and pepper to taste. Fold in Parmesan, chopped spinach, bacon, and ¾ cup of mozzarella.
3. Sprinkle the remaining ¼ cup of mozzarella after transferring the dip to a baking dish. Bake for 25-30 minutes until golden and fizzy.
4. Serve with crostini.

Keto Bread

Ingredients:

6 large eggs
½ tsp cream of tartar
¼ c (½ stick) butter (melted and cooled)
1 ½ c almond flour (finely ground)
1 tbsp baking powder
½ tsp kosher salt

Procedure:

1. Preheat oven to 375°. Prepare an 8"-x-4" loaf pan with parchment paper. Separate egg whites and egg yolks.
2. Mix cream of tartar and egg whites in a large bowl. Whip until stiff peaks form using a hand mixer.
3. Beat yolks with melted butter, baking powder, almond flour, and salt in a separate large bowl using a hand mixer. Blend ⅓ of the whipped egg wash until thoroughly combined, then blend the rest.
4. Pour the mixture into loaf pan and smooth top. Bake for 30 minutes, or until top is slightly golden and a toothpick inserted comes out clean. Let cool 30 minutes before slicing.

Bacon Zucchini Fries

Ingredients:

cooking spray
4 zucchini (cut into wedges)
16 strips bacon

ranch for serving

Procedure:

1. Preheat oven to 425°. Spray the parchment sheet with a cooking spray. Wrap each cut zucchini in bacon and place on the sprayed baking sheet.
2. Bake for 35 minutes until the bacon is cooked through and crispy. Serve with ranch.

Cheese Ball Bites

Ingredients:

8 slices bacon
1 ½ oz (8-oz) blocks cream cheese softened
1 c shredded cheddar
1 tsp garlic powder
1 tsp paprika
kosher salt
black pepper (freshly ground)
⅓ c chives (freshly chopped)
⅓ c pecans (finely chopped)
18 pretzels sticks

Procedure:

1. Cook the bacon for 8 minutes until crispy in a large nonstick pan. Dry on a paper towel-lined plate, then finely chop. Set aside.

2. In the meantime, stir together cream cheese, cheddar cheese, garlic powder, and paprika in a large bowl. Season with salt and pepper to taste. To form mixture into 18 small balls use a cookie scoop and transfer to a parchment–lined baking sheet. Refrigerate until firm, 1 hour.
3. Mix together bacon, chives, and pecans in a empty bowl.
4. In a bacon-chive-pecan mixture, roll the balls. Place in pretzel stick into each ball. Before serving, let it sit for 15 minutes. (If not serving right away, loosely cover with plastic wrap and return to fridge.

Roast Turkey

Ingredients:

1 12-14 lb. whole turkey (neck and giblets removed)
kosher salt
black pepper (freshly ground)
1 onion (cut into wedges)
1 bunch thyme
rosemary sprigs (small handful)
1 sage leaves (small handful)
1 head garlic (halved crosswise)
½ c butter (melted)
2 c chicken broth

Procedure:

1. Preheat oven to 450°. Place the rack to the lower third part of your oven. Pat dry the turkey with paper towels and season the cavity generously with salt and pepper. Stuff the cavity with rosemary, onion, thyme, garlic, and sage. Bind the legs together with kitchen twine and tuck the wing tips under the body.
2. Brush butter all over turkey then season with salt and pepper. Put turkey breast side up inside a large pan on a roasting rack. Pour chicken broth into the pan. Transfer to oven and immediately lower oven heat to 350°.
3. Grease with the juices on the bottom of the pan every 30 to 45 minutes. Roast for about 3-4 hours, or until the juices of the meat run clear. The meat temperature should be 165°.
4. Use aluminum foil to cover the cooked turkey and let sit for 20 minutes before carving.

Loaded Zucchini Skins

Ingredients:

½ lb bacon
4 large zucchini
2 tbsp extra-virgin olive oil
½ tsp chili powder
¼ tsp cumin
kosher salt
black pepper (freshly ground)
2 c cheddar (shredded)

1 c sour cream
2 green onions (sliced)

Procedure:

1. Preheat oven to 400°. Cook bacon for 8-10 minutes until crispy, then transfer to a paper towel-lined plate to drain and chop into small pieces.
2. Cut the zucchinis in half lengthwise. Scoop out seeds from the insides using a large metal spoon. After that cut each zucchini in half, then 3 to 4 cuts.
3. Toss the large baking sheet with olive oil then transfer zucchini in it. Sprinkle with cumin, chili powder, pepper and salt.
4. Bake until slightly tender, about 5 minutes. Top each piece of zucchini with cheese and bacon.
5. Go back to oven and bake until cheese is bubbly and zucchini is tender, about 10 minutes more. Garnish with sour cream and green onions.

Loaded Cauliflower Bake

Ingredients:

2 small heads cauliflower (cut into florets)
2 tbsp butter
3 cloves garlic (minced)
3 tbsp all-purpose flour
2 c whole milk
2 oz cream cheese (softened)
1 ½ c shredded cheddar (divided)

kosher salt
black pepper (freshly ground)
6 slices bacon (cooked and crumbled)
¼ c green onions (sliced)

Procedure:

1. Preheat oven to 350°. Shrink the cauliflower in a large pot of salted boiling water for 3 minutes. Let it sit, drain and squeeze cauliflower of water.
2. To make cheese sauce: Melt butter in a large pan. Add garlic and cook for a minute, then add flour and stir until golden, 2 minutes. Add milk and bring to a low simmer, then add cream cheese, whisking until combined. Remove from heat and stir in 1 cup cheddar until melted, then season with salt and pepper.
3. Add drained cauliflower in a 9"-x-13" dish. Put cheese sauce on top and stir until combined thoroughly. Mix the ingredients 1 tablespoon each, cooked bacon and green onions until combined, then top with remaining cheddar, bacon, and green onions.
4. Bake for about 30 minutes until cauliflower gets tender, and cheese is melty.

Cheesy Bacon Butternut Squash
Ingredients:

2 lb butternut squash cut into 1" pieces (peeled)

2 tbsp olive oil
2 cloves garlic (minced)
2 tbsp thyme (chopped)
kosher salt
black pepper (freshly ground)
½ lb bacon (chopped)
1 ½ c mozzarella (shredded)
½ c parmesan (freshly grated)
parsley for garnish (chopped fresh)

Procedure:

1. Preheat oven to 425°. Toss butternut squash with garlic, olive oil, and thyme in a large ovenproof skillet (or in a large baking dish). Sprinkle with pepper and salt, then spread bacon on top.
2. Bake for 20 to 25 minutes until the squash is tender and the bacon is cooked.
3. Take the skillet out of oven and top with mozzarella and Parmesan. Bake for another 5 to 10 minutes, or until the cheese is melty.
4. Garnish with parsley and serve warm.

Bacon Pecan Cheese Log

(Keto Bread perfect match)

Ingredients:

8 oz cream cheese (softened)

⅔ c white cheddar
1 tsp garlic powder
kosher salt
black pepper (freshly ground)
12 slices bacon (cooked and crumbled, divided)
½ c toasted pecans (chopped and divided)
½ c chives (chopped and divided)

Procedure:

1. Combine cream cheese with cheddar, half the bacon, garlic powder, half the pecans, and half the chives in a large bowl. Season with pepper and salt. Mix until well incorporated.
2. In an empty bowl place a piece of plastic wrap and form into a log shape with your hands. Place in the refrigerator to harden slightly.
3. Combine the remaining chives, bacon, and pecans in a large plate. Stir so that they are distributed evenly on the plate. Take the cheese log out of the refrigerator and roll in a mixture. Press more toppings with your hands if needed. Place on a serving dish with crackers or vegetables for dipping.

Crudite Turkey

Ingredients:

For Turkey:
1 lettuce (butterhead)
1 16-oz baby carrots

1 green bell pepper (cut into slices and bottom removed)
1 red bell pepper (cut into slices)
1 yellow bell pepper (cut into slices, and one triangle for the beak)
1 large cucumber (cut into rounds)
1 olive (sliced)

For Dip:
8 oz cream cheese (softened)
1 c sour cream
½ c parsley leaves
½ c dill
2 tbsp chives
1 tbsp fresh lemon juice
1 tsp garlic powder
kosher salt
black pepper (freshly ground)

Procedure:

1. Place a layer of butterhead lettuce into a large plate. Then on the top half of the plate add a layer of baby carrots. Set bell peppers just below in a half circle pattern right after the carrots. Below the peppers, create a large circle below the peppers, overlapping the cucumbers. At the bottom place a green bell pepper in the center of the cucumbers. For the nose, topped with one piece of yellow pepper and for the eyes put two slices of olive.

2. Combine sour cream, cream cheese, parsley, dill, chives, lemon juice, and garlic powder in a small food processor.
3. Season with pepper and salt and blend until smooth. Pour into bowl. Serve with turkey crudite.

Brussels Sprout Chips

Ingredients:

½ kg brussels sprouts
2 tbsp extra-virgin olive oil
kosher salt
black pepper (ground)
¼ cup parmesan (grated)

Procedure:

1. Preheat oven to 400°F.
2. Cut off each Brussels sprout stem end. Pickoff all leaves from the bud using your hands. The tough outer leaves should fall off naturally.
3. In a large rimmed baking sheet, transfer the leaves. Toss with olive oil until each piece is coated evenly on both sides. Season with salt and pepper.
4. On the baking sheet (single layer), spread the Brussels sprouts evenly. Drizzle with Parmesan cheese and bake for about 10-12 minutes, until the Brussels sprouts are crispy and have darkened. (It will become more crispy as they cool.)

5. If desired, drizzle with more Parmesan and chill for at least 10 minutes before serving.

Roasted Asparagus Wrapped in Ham

Ingredients:

½ kg thick asparagus spears (woody ends trimmed)
½ kg smoked lean ham (packaged ham that's cut into same-size pieces will work best)

Procedure:

1. Preheat oven to 400F/205C.
2. Using non-stick spray, spray a baking sheet. (All the wrapped asparagus can cook at once if you have two or more baking sheets and room in the oven.)
3. Make all the pieces the same size by trimming the woody ends of asparagus spears.
4. Roll each piece of asparagus by a slice of ham around, securing with a toothpick inserted horizontally so the portion of asparagus will lay flat on the baking sheet.
5. Line the asparagus on the sprayed baking sheet, staggering the pieces so you'll be able to turn them.
6. Put the ham wrapped asparagus in the oven and roast it for 8-10 minutes on the first side, or until the ham become lightly brown.
7. Turn asparagus pieces on the other side. Roast for 5-7 minutes more on the second side, until

asparagus is barely tender-crisp and ham is lightly brown on both sides.

8. Repeat the steps on the remaining asparagus pieces if you're only using one baking sheet.
9. Serve hot. Add mustard dipping sauce on the side (optional but highly suggested).

Roasted Mushrooms with Garlic & Thyme
Ingredients:

16 open cup mushrooms (even-sized and stalks cut level)
3 tbsp vegetable or olive oil
2 cloves garlic (thinly chopped)
3 tbsp butter (softened unsalted)
2 tbsp fresh thyme (chopped)
½ tsp garlic powder
¼ cup almond meal
1½ tbsp lemon juice
salt and ground black pepper to taste

Procedure:

1. Preheat the oven to 400°F. In hot oil, lightly fry the mushrooms, cap-side down for 2-3 minutes.
2. Align the mushrooms in a 9x13 cooking dish (or whatever rectangular ovenproof dish you have on hand) with the stalks facing upwards.
3. Mix the softened butter, garlic, thyme, lemon juice, and seasoning in a small bowl.

4. Put a little garlic butter on to each mushroom, then lightly press the breadcrumbs on top.
5. Immediately bake in the oven for 15 minutes or golden around the mushroom cap.

Crustless Low-Carb Pumpkin Pie

Ingredients:

1 can 425 g organic pumpkin
1 cup coconut cream
⅔ cup erythritol crystals
3 extra large organic eggs
2 tsp pumpkin pie spice

Procedure:

1. Preheat oven to 350 °F (175 °C).
2. Grease a 10-inch baking dish or pie pan generously with butter. Set aside.
3. In a large bowl place all ingredients. Stir until smooth and without a single lump.
4. Pour the mixture in the greased pie pan.
5. Bake for an hour, or until the center of the pie appears slightly higher than the edges.
6. Remove from oven and let cool completely.
7. Refrigerate overnight. Serve the next day with whipped cream.

Pumpkin Pie Pudding

Ingredients:

For the pudding:
½ cup coconut cream (canned)
¼ cup pumpkin (canned)
1 tbsp maple syrup
½ tsp cinnamon
¼ tsp ground nutmeg
¼ tsp ground ginger
⅛ tsp sea salt

For the whipped topping:
1 tbsp coconut cream
½ tsp maple syrup
⅛ tsp vanilla extract

Procedure:

For the pudding:
1. For the pumpkin pudding, mix all the ingredients in a small bowl. Pour into your desired serving glass.

For the whipped topping:
1. Mix all of the whipped cream toppings in a small bowl. Pour over the first layer. To set coconut cream better, refrigerate for 30 minutes or more.

Fudgy Macadamia Chocolate Fat Bombs
Ingredients:

2 oz cocoa butter

2 tbsp cocoa powder (unsweetened)

2 tbsp swerve

4 oz macadamias (chopped)

¼ cup heavy cream or coconut oil for dairy free option

Procedure:

1. Melt cocoa butter in a small saucepan in a bath of water.
2. Add cocoa powder to the pan.
3. Now add the Swerve and stir until all ingredients are well blended and melted.
4. Add macadamias and stir in well.
5. Put cream, mix well and bring back to temperature.
6. Pour in molds or paper candy cups.
7. Let it cool. Place in the fridge to harden.
8. Keep at room temperature, with a slightly softer consistency than chocolate.

Chapter 11: Keto Menu Guide for a Guilt-Free Thanksgiving Feast (Thanksgiving Appetizers)

Bacon and Butter Wrapped Asparagus

Ingredients:

bacon
asparagus (fresh or frozen)
sea salt (coarse)
pepper
garlic
salt
butter

Procedure:

1. Preheat oven to 400°F.
2. For easy cleanup cover a baking pan in aluminum foil.
3. If you have thick asparagus stems, make a bundle of 2, for the thinner ones maybe a bunch of 3 or Start wrapping the bacon at the end and wrap bacon around tightly up to the tips.
4. Spread over prepared pan, leaving a couple of inches between each one so that the heat can cook it each bundle evenly.

5. Sprinkle bundles with sea salt and pepper.
6. In a small bowl melt a couple of teaspoons of butter and whisk in a ¼ teaspoon of salt and garlic and drizzle over each bundle.
7. Bake for 15 minutes then turn the broiler on to give it an extra crispy finish.

Cheesy Cheddar Bites

Ingredients:

½ c cheddar cheese (shredded)
¼ c mozzarella cheese (shredded)
¼ c parmesan cheese (grated)
½ c almond flour
2 eggs
¼ tsp garlic powder
¼ tsp parsley flakes
salt and pepper to taste

Procedure:

1. Preheat the oven to 400°F.
2. In a mixing bowl crack 2 eggs, season with salt and pepper, and beat with a whisk.
3. Add all three kinds of cheese, almond flour, garlic powder, and parsley flakes to the eggs and stir until a dough forms.
4. Divide the dough into 8 slices and roll each part into a ball.

5. Bake on a parchment-lined baking sheet for 14 minutes until golden brown and slightly crispy.

Sausage and Cranberry Stuffed Mushrooms with Sage

Ingredients:

8 oz sausage (ground)
30-35 large white button mushrooms (stems removed)
½ cup chopped apples (in tiny pieces, or even shredded, skinned cored)
¼ cup chopped leeks
¼ cup chopped pecans
3 tbsp olive oil
⅓ cup cranberries (chopped dried)
2 tbsp fresh sage (chopped)
2 eggs beaten
1 clove garlic (minced)

Procedure:

1. Preheat the oven to 350 degrees. Grease lightly a large baking sheet, set aside.
2. Heat a large skillet to medium-high. Spread 2 tbsp oil, put the sausage and start cooking. After 2 to 3 minutes, add in apples, pecans, and leeks. Saute for another 4 to 5 minutes, or until sausage is cooked thoroughly. To avoid the sausage of having big chunks, continue breaking it apart while cooking.

3. Pour mixture into a medium-sized bowl. Add in fresh sage, cranberries, and eggs. Stir around, to mix all the ingredients well.
4. Combine the extra oil with freshly crushed garlic. Place the mushrooms inside the baking sheet. Brush each mushroom caps with oil/garlic mixture.
5. Spoon the mixture in each mushroom cap.
6. Place inside the oven. Bake for 25 minutes, or until mushrooms achieve the brown color. Serve hot!

Easy Buffalo Chicken Dip

Ingredients:

3 cups chicken (cooked shredded)
¾ cup blue cheese dressing
¾ cup franks red hot sauce
12 oz cream cheese
1 cup mozzarella cheese (shredded)
¼ cup jalapenos (optional, for topping)

Procedure:

1. Heat the saucepan to medium and then add cream cheese and hot sauce to a medium heat saucepan.
2. Once thoroughly combined stir in the blue cheese dressing and chicken.
3. Once fully incorporated, slowly mix in ¾ cup of the mozzarella cheese.

4. Transfer mixture to an 8x8 baking dish once thoroughly mixed. Layer the rest of the mozzarella cheese on top.
5. Bake for about 15 mins. in a 350° oven.
6. Serve warm and enjoy!

Turkey Meatballs

Ingredients:

1 tbsp coconut oil for pan
1 lb ground turkey (breast)
1 egg
1 yellow onion (peeled and trimmed and grated)
¼ cup almond flour (plus ½ cup almond flour, divided)
2-3 tbsp frank hot sauce
1 tsp italian seasoning
2 tbsp italian parsley (dried)
¼ tsp sea salt
⅛ tsp black pepper (ground)
sugar-free marinara sauce

Procedure:

1. Preheat oven to 400°F
2. Wrap baking sheet with foil {for easy clean up}
3. In a large bowl combine turkey, ¼ cup almond flour and remaining ingredients to ground black pepper. Combine thoroughly with a fork, or use your hands, it is easier using hands.

4. Place remaining ½ cup of almond flour in a small bowl.
5. Start forming meatballs into 2" balls.
6. Roll balls in almond flour, gently shake meatballs to loosen excess almond flour.
7. Heat pan over medium heat and melt coconut oil.
8. Drop meatballs into pan spacing 2" apart. Let brown 3-4 minutes and flip to brown additional side 3-4 minutes. I use a large spoon to flip
9. Place browned meatballs on baking sheet, and continue until all meatballs are browned.
10. Place cookie sheet in oven and bake meatballs for 25 minutes.
11. Meanwhile heat up Marinara sauce according to directions.
12. Remove meatballs and place into a large serving bowl, top with marinara sauce, serve and enjoy.

Turkey Meatballs

Ingredients:

1 tbsp coconut oil
1 lb ground turkey (breast part)
1 egg
1 yellow onion (grated)
¼ cup almond flour (plus ½ cup almond flour, separated)
2-3 tbsp frank hot sauce
1 tsp italian seasoning
2 tbsps dried italian parsley

¼ tsp sea salt
⅛ tsp black pepper (ground)
sugar-free marinara sauce

Procedure:

1. Preheat oven to 400°F
2. Wrap baking sheet with foil
3. Combine ground turkey, ¼ cup almond flour and remaining ingredients to ground black pepper in a large bowl. Mix well with a fork, but it's a lot easier to use your hands.
4. Pour remaining ½ cup of almond flour in a small bowl.
5. Start forming meatballs into 2" balls.
6. Roll meatballs in almond flour, gently shake meatballs to loosen excess almond flour.
7. Thaw coconut oil in a pan over medium heat.
8. Put meatballs into pan spacing 2 inches apart. Let it brown 3 to 4 minutes and flip to brown additional side 3-4 minutes. Use a large spoon to flip
9. Place cooked meatballs on a baking sheet, and continue until all meatballs are brown.
10. Place cookie sheet in the oven and bake meatballs for 25 minutes.
11. Meanwhile, heat Marinara sauce according to directions.
12. Remove meatballs from the oven and put into a large serving bowl, top with marinara sauce, serve and enjoy.

Low-Carb Cheesy Zucchini Chips

Ingredients:

4 small zucchinis
1 to 1 ½ cups parmesan cheese
low sugar spaghetti sauce for dipping (optional)

Procedure:

1. Cut each zucchini into slices that are about ¼ inch thick.
2. Prepare a large baking sheet with tin foil or parchment paper.
3. Spread out the sliced zucchini rounds on to the large baking sheet and don't worry too much if there is little space between each one.
4. Now sprinkle your cheese evenly over each Zucchini round covering each one.
5. Bake on 425 degrees for about 15 to 20 minutes or until the cheese turns a golden brown color.
6. You can serve it with a small amount of spaghetti sauce to add even more flavor too! We do that often as well.
7. Serve warm and Enjoy!

Stuffed Mushrooms

Ingredients:

1 lb jones no sugar pork sausage roll sausage
¼ cup onion (finely chopped)
1 garlic clove (minced)
1 pack reduced-fat cream cheese (8 oz)
¼ cup parmesan cheese (shredded)
⅓ cup bread crumbs (seasoned)
3 tsp basil (dried)
1-½ tsp parsley-flakes (dried)
30 large fresh mushrooms about 1-½ pounds (stems removed)
3 tbsps butter (melted)

Procedure:

1. Preheat oven to 400°F.
2. In a large pan, cook onion, garlic, and sausage, onion over medium heat 6 to 8 minutes or until sausage become light brown, and onion are tender, breaking up sausage into crumbles; drain.
3. Add cream cheese and Parmesan cheese. Cook and stir until melted. Stir in bread crumbs, basil, and parsley.
4. Meanwhile, grease 15x10x1-inches baking pan. Place mushroom caps, stem side up. Brush with butter. Spoon sausage mixture into mushroom caps.
5. Uncover it and bake for 12-15 minutes or until mushrooms are tender.

Antipasto Skewers

Ingredients:

8 prosciutto (slices)
16 ciliegine (1 inch) mozzarella balls
16 sun-dried tomatoes in oil
16 basil leaves

Procedure:

1. Cut prosciutto slices in half.
2. Fold up prosciutto and place one sun-dried tomato, one basil leaf, and one mozzarella ball on top of it.
3. Skewer with a toothpick.

Antipasto Salad with Easy Italian Dressing
Ingredients:

Salad:
1 large head or 2 hearts romaine (chopped)
4 oz prosciutto cut in strips
4 oz salami or pepperoni (cubed)
½ cup artichoke hearts (sliced)
½ cup olives-mix of black and green
½ cup hot or sweet peppers (pickled or roasted)
italian dressing to taste

Italian Dressing:
1 tbsp flat leaf parsley (freshly chopped)
1 tsp dried oregano
1 clove garlic with a garlic press (minced)
½ tsp sea salt or more to taste

¼ tsp black pepper (freshly cracked)

¼ c red wine vinegar

¾ c organic extra virgin olive oil

Procedure:

Salad:

1. In a large bowl combine all ingredients. Toss with Italian dressing.

Italian Dressing:

1. Shaking Method: Put all ingredients to a bottle or jar with a tight lid cover and shake firmly until well incorporated.
2. Whisking Method: Put all ingredients to a mixing bowl and whisk until the ingredients come together.
3. Taste and adjust seasonings if needed.

Thanksgiving Side Dishes

Cauliflower Stuffing

Ingredients:

4 tbsp butter

1 onion (chopped)

2 large carrots (peeled and chopped)

2 celery stalks (chopped or thinly sliced)

1 small head cauliflower (chopped)

1 c mushrooms (chopped)

kosher salt

freshly ground black pepper

¼ c fresh parsley (chopped)
2 tbsp fresh rosemary (chopped)
1 tbsp fresh sage (chopped)
½ c vegetable or chicken broth

Procedure:

1. Using a medium-heat large pan, melt the butter.
2. Add and sauté the onion, carrot, and celery for 7 to 8 minutes.
3. Add the cauliflower and mushrooms and season with salt and pepper. Cook until tender for at least 8 to 10 minutes or more.
4. Add the parsley, rosemary, and sage. Stir until combined.
5. Pour over the vegetable broth or chicken broth and cover with a lid. Cover for 15 minutes until tender and liquid are absorbed.
6. Serve.

Mushroom, Bacon and Cauliflower Casserole

Ingredients:

8 oz bacon (chopped)
1 cup onion (diced)
1 tbsp thyme (fresh)
6 garlic cloves (minced)
½ tsp salt
½ tsp ground pepper
12 oz cremini mushrooms (sliced)

4 oz shiitake mushrooms (sliced)
4 cups cauliflower crumbles
¼ cup chicken bone broth
1 cup spinach (fresh)
2 tsp coconut aminos

Procedure:

1. Preheat the oven to 375 degrees F.
2. Make cauliflower crumbles by adding the florets to a food processor and pulse until broken down into coarse crumbles. Set aside.
3. In a deep pot, cook the bacon pieces over medium-high heat until crisp.
4. Remove the bacon from the pot. Reserve 1 tbsp drippings in the pot. Set aside the bacon.
5. Retake the pot to medium-high heat and add the onion, garlic, and thyme to the drippings. Cook for 3 minutes until it turned light brown and tender.
6. Now, add the mushrooms, salt, and pepper. Cook for 10 minutes while stirring occasionally.
7. Cook the cauliflower crumbles and broth for 5 minutes.
8. Add the spinach, bacon and coconut aminos. Stir until the spinach become wilted then remove from heat.
9. Transfer to a 2-quart baking dish.
10. Cover with aluminum foil and bake for at least 15 minutes.

11. Remove the foil and bake for an additional 10 minutes. Serve warm.

Sausage and Herb Stuffing

Ingredients:

¾ pound turkey sausage (or pork breakfast sausage)
¼ cup celery (finely chopped)
¼ cup red onion (chopped)
2 eggs
2 cups cauliflower (coarsely chopped)
½ cup yellow squash (diced)
½ cup Parmesan (grated)
1 tbsp parsley leaves (chopped)
3 tbsp sage leaves (fresh, chopped)
3 tbsp thyme leaves (fresh, chopped)
1 tbsp garlic (minced)
⅛ tsp salt
⅛ tsp ground black pepper (fresh)

Procedure:

1. Preheat the oven to 350 degrees F.
2. Prepare the sausage by removing from casing and crumble it into a pan over medium heat.
3. Put the celery and onion to the pan with sausage and cook. Stir until browned. Drain the fat if necessary.
4. Beat the eggs in a small bowl.

5. Using a spoon, mix the sausage mixture and all the remaining ingredients.
6. Pour the mixture to the baking dish and bake until hot and browned
7. Serve immediately.

Sugar-Free Cranberry Sauce

Ingredients:

1 12oz bag of cranberries (fresh)
¾ cup water
¼ cup or more granulated erythritol
30 drops stevia (extract)

Procedure:

1. Using a medium saucepan, boil the cranberries, water, and erythritol over medium-high heat.
2. Reduce the heat to medium-low and continue to cook.
3. Stir occasionally until the cranberries pop.
4. Remove from heat and stir in stevia.
5. Let it cool in the pan.
6. Put it in a glass jar and let it store in the fridge.

Mashed Cauliflower

Ingredients:

1 bag cauliflower florets (16 oz, frozen)

1 tsp garlic clove (crushed)
1 ½ tbsp coconut oil
½ cup coconut milk
salt and black pepper to taste
1 tbsp plus 2 teaspoons chopped chives (dried)

Procedure:

1. Cook the cauliflower until it's very soft but not waterlogged.
2. Using a microwaveable bowl or saucepan, heat the garlic, coconut oil, coconut milk, salt, and pepper for about 1 minute and set aside.
3. Purée the cauliflower in the bowl of a food processor scrapping down the sides.
4. Add the coconut milk to the processor along with one tablespoon of chives and process for 10 seconds.
5. Taste and adjust with seasonings.
6. Sprinkle the remaining chives before serving.

Simple Herb and Garlic Roasted Turkey Breast
Ingredients:

3 lbs turkey breast (skin on - bone in)
2 cloves garlic (minced)
1 tsp dried thyme
1 tsp dried rosemary
1 tsp dried sage leaves
1 tsp salt

½ tsp ground black pepper
2 tbsp extra virgin olive oil

Procedure:

1. Preheat the oven to 350 degrees.
2. Rinse the turkey and pat dry.
3. Using a small bowl, combine the herbs, garlic, salt, olive oil, and pepper.
4. Rub the mixture all over the turkey.
5. Place it in the roasting pan.
6. Roast the turkey to 350 degrees for 45 minutes to 1 hour. You can use a thermometer and insert it into the thickest part of the breast but not touching the bone until it reaches 165 degrees,
7. Once cooked, cover the turkey with foil and rest for at least 10 minutes.
8. Carve and serve.

Easy Crock-Pot Ham

Ingredients:

1 ham (7 pounds fits in a 6-quart crock-pot)
¼ cup apple juice
¼ cup honey
cinnamon, cloves, or other flavorings to taste
water (enough to cover the bottom of your slow cooker)

Procedure:

1. Start by covering the bottom of your slow cooker with water.
2. Insert the ham.
3. Create an apple juice/honey mixture including the seasonings and pour it over the ham.
4. Cover and cook for 8 to 12 hours depending on the size of the ham.
5. Check it occasionally. You can scoop the juices and pour it over the ham.
6. You can start cooking this the night before the occasion so you'll be ready for an early afternoon feast.

Prosciutto-Wrapped Whole Roasted Beef Tenderloin

Ingredients:

1 4 lbs trimmed whole beef tenderloin (raw, tail removed)
1 tbsp raw garlic (chopped or crushed)
1 tbsp olive oil
1 tbsp kosher salt
¼ tsp ground black pepper
1 tbsp fresh parsley (chopped)
4 oz deli sliced prosciutto

Procedure:

1. Preheat the oven to 425 degrees (F).
2. On a clean cutting board, place the tenderloin.
3. Combine the garlic, olive oil, salt, pepper, fresh parsley in a small bowl.
4. Start rubbing the garlic mixture all over the tenderloin.
5. Then gently wrap the tenderloin. It should overlap the ribbons of prosciutto.
6. Place the tenderloin on a roasting pan.
7. Now, place it in the preheated oven. If you want it rare, set for 26 - 28 minutes. 30 minutes for medium rare, and 35 to 40 minutes to make it well done.
8. Remove it from the oven and rest for at least 10 minutes before slicing.
9. Serve it the way you want maybe warm or cold.

Lemon Garlic Roast Chicken

Ingredients:

1 whole chicken (giblets removed)
3 tbsp bacon fat (at room temperature, not melted)
4 – 6 cloves of garlic (peeled)
1 lemon
2 sprigs fresh rosemary
salt to taste

Procedure:

1. Prepare the chicken - if it's from the fridge, remove it at least half and hour before cooking.
2. Lay the chicken on a plate line with paper towels to absorb any excess moisture.
3. Using a food processor, chop the garlic and add the bacon fat on a preheated oven (475 F). Whip the two ingredients until combined.
4. Zest the lemon and mix it into the garlic fat mixture.
5. Now, using your hands place the chicken into a roasting dish and separate the skin from the breast.
6. Use two-thirds of the garlic-fat mixture, filling it under the chicken skin.
7. Put the chicken skin back into position and spread the fat on the breast.
8. Squeeze the lemon juice over the chicken and add the rosemary sprigs.
9. Using the remaining fat, rub it over outside the chicken skin. Put salt and pepper to taste.
10. Set the chicken again on the oven positioning in the middle. Turn the oven down to 400 F.
11. Roast the chicken until done. It may take 55 minutes to 1 hour and 5 minutes.
12. Remove the chicken from the oven, rest, cover for 15 minutes before carving.

Easy Brined Smoked Turkey Breast

Ingredients:

1 whole turkey (breastbone - in)
4 cups water

½ onion (chopped)
2 stalks celery (chopped)
1 tsp mustard seeds
1 tsp garlic (crushed)
2 bay leaves
1 tsp fennel seeds
¼ tsp cayenne
2 tbsp salt
4 tbsp sugar (brown)

Procedure:

1. First, split the turkey breast into two pieces.
2. Then mix all the other ingredients in a bowl.
3. In a large container, add the two breasts and pour the brining mixture over the top. Refrigerate overnight.
4. Take out from the container and pat dry.
5. Place the turkey in the smoker and adjust the temperature between 200 and 225 degrees F.
6. Smoke it for at least 5 hours or until the roast reaches 170 degrees F with a meat thermometer.
7. Let it sit for 10 minutes then carve.

Part 2

Mashed potato sumpreme

READY TO EAT IN: 30 min
MAKES: 6
GOOD STUFF 2 KNOWN: *
    FOR POTATOES: Calories: **293** Total Fat: 5g Cholesterol: 12**mg**
  FOR GRAVY: Calories: **151** Total Fat: **11g** Cholesterol: 20**mg**

SERVE FOR: Dinner

    INGREDIENTS

FOR MASHED POTATOES:

6 red potatoes (washed thoroughly)
1 head cauliflower (chopped)
1 tablespoon extra-virgin olive oil
2 tablespoon tahini
1 tablespoon vegan butter
¼ teaspoon sea salt
¼ teaspoon cayenne powder
¼ teaspoon black pepper
1 ripe avocado (diced)

FOR MUSHROOM GRAVY:

8 ounces baby portobello mushrooms (sliced)
1 tablespoon shallots (minced)
3 tablespoons unbleached flour

2 tablespoons vegan butter
1 tablespoon extra-virgin olive oil
1 clove garlic (minced)
1 cup almond milk (any non-dairy milk)
   pinch sea salt (to taste)
   pinch black pepper (to taste)

DIRECTIONS

FOR MASHED POTATOES:

In a large saucepan, cover potatoes with water and bring to a boil. Reduce heat to a low boil and then add in the cauliflower and cover.

Once both are soft and cooked through, drain the water (save about 2 tablespoons) then transfer into a large bowl. Add in the ripe avocado and mash with a potato masher until desired texture is reached (I like chucks of potatoes). To avoid green mashed potatoes just add in the diced avocados to the finished product.

Add in the remaining ingredients for the potatoes (salt, pepper, cayenne, butter, tahini, oil and the saved water). Blend well using a fork and cover until time to serve. (if they are too loose for you add a little flour, if too dry add a little non-dairy milk)

FOR MUSHROOM GRAVY:

In skillet over medium heat add in the oil and garlic. Once the garlic is light brown, add the vegan butter. When the butter is melted then add the shallots and mushrooms, stirring frequently. Cook until the mushrooms are soft and brown (or until most of their liquid has evaporated).

Stir in the flour with a whisk and reduce heat to medium. Cook for another minute or two.

Slowly add in the almond milk (veggie broth if a oilier texture is desired) while whisking to reduce clumps. Reduce heat to simmer and continue to stir until it reaches desired thickness (about 8 minutes). If it appears too thin, add a touch more flour and whisk. If it's too thick, add more fake milk or broth. Serve over the Mashed Potato Supreme or your whole plate of food.

MAKE IT BETTER:
Try adding vegan sour cream to the potato mixture for a creamier texture. Also, for something a little tastier you can saute onions and tomatoes in 2 tablespoons of olive oil then add in the potato mixture and let fry on a low heat until the potatoes appear light brown. To save time and space throw it all in a slow cooker.

GOES WELL WITH:
Dinner – Any barbequed fake meat, a green veggie like asparagus and a tasty corn relish.

167

COMPLETE NUTRITIONAL VALUES: **

FOR POTATOES:

Total Fat **12g** 18 % **(Sat Fat 3g 15 %)** Total Carbohydrates **43g** 14 % Fiber **8g** 32 %

Sugars **5g** --- Cholesterol **5mg** 2 % Sodium **208mg** 9 % Protein **7g** 15 %

FOR GRAVY:

Total Fat **11g** 17 % **(Sat Fat 5g 25 %)** Total Carbohydrates **10g** 3 % Fiber **1g** 4 %

Sugars **4g** --- Cholesterol **20**mg 7 % Sodium **146**mg 6 % Protein **5g** 10 %

* (nutritional facts are per serving and accuracy is not certain)

** **(**percentages based on 2000 calories diet, data may be incomplete or calculations inaccurate)

Turkeyless loaf

READY TO EAT IN: 120 min
MAKES: 6
GOOD STUFF 2 KNOWN: * Calories: **387** Total Fat: **11g** Cholesterol: **1mg**
SERVE FOR: Dinner

INGREDIENTS

FOR FILLING:

4 ounces Jewish Rye (vegan) bread (cubed like croutons)

4 ounces celery (chopped)

6 ounces mushrooms (sliced)

6 ounces red onion (chopped)

¼ cup cranberries (dried)

½ cup walnuts (chopped)

¼ teaspoon thyme (dried or fresh)

¼ teaspoon sage

¼ teaspoon black pepper

1 teaspoon flax seed (grounded)

1 tablespoon vegan soy sauce

½ cup water

FOR SEITAN:

2 cups wheat gluten

1 cup northern beans

½ cup quinoa flakes

12 ounces vegetable broth

1 clove garlic (minced)

¼ cup nutritional yeast

½ teaspoon thyme

½ teaspoon basil

½ teaspoon sage

1 teaspoon flax seed

1 tablespoon tahini

2 tablespoons vegan soy sauce

FOR BROTH:

½   cup vegetable broth
½   teaspoon sesame oil
1   tablespoon vegan soy sauce
        DIRECTIONS

FOR FILLING:

Saute onions and celery in a non-stick skillet until onions become translucent. Add in the mushrooms, thyme, sage, and black pepper then cover. Cook for about 3 minutes or until the mushrooms release their juices. Add the remaining filling ingredients along with enough water to moisten the stuffing but not make it mushy. Remove from heat and keep covered.

FOR SEITAN:

In a mixing bowl combine the dry ingredients (wheat gluten, thyme, basil, sage, flax seed, quinoa flakes, tahini and nutritional yeast) Place the remaining ingredients (broth, white beans, soy sauce, and garlic) in a blender and process until liquefied. Make a well in the center of the dry ingredients, and add the blended mixture. Then stir until gluten is completely moistened.

FOR BROTH:

Using a small sauce pan on low heat combine the broth ingredients. Let them cook together until hot but do not bring to a boil.

FOR MAKING THE LOAF:

Preheat the oven to 400° F. Lightly oil a rectangular baking dish, 11-13 inches long and 6-8 inches wide. Line your work surface with waxed paper. Place the dough in the center and cover it with plastic wrap. Roll out the seitan mixture, making sure that it is the same thickness in all places, until it is about 9"×13". Spread the stuffing evenly (leave a one inch margin on all sides). Lift up the plastic wrap on one of the long edges and roll the seitan up like a jelly roll (arrange the stuffing in a horizontal line across the middle of the seitan and bring one long edge up and over it to the other side). Pinch the ends sealed first and then pinch well to seal the long seam. To avoid leaks make sure that the edges are completely sealed and no gaps or stuffing shows. Lift the seitan roll carefully and place seam-side down in the prepared casserole dish. Pour the prepared broth (soy-sesame concoction) over it and cover **tightly** with aluminum foil. After baking for 25 minutes, remove from oven and baste with broth. Recover it tightly and bake for another 25 minutes the remove and baste again. Return to oven uncovered for about 20 more minutes. To keep it moist continue to baste it 2 or 3 times while it is cooking. Cook until the top is firm and brown and the broth has evaporated.
Remove from the oven and let cool for 5-10 minutes. Slice into preferred thickness and serve.

MAKE IT BETTER:

Try covering it with your favorite gravy.

GOES WELL WITH:
Lunch – Use in a grilled sandwich with vegan mayonnaise, tomato slices and onions. Use your imagination, make your favorite sandwich using the loaf as a meat substitute.

Dinner – Put on the side of any stir fry or/and a hearty vegan soup. Also can be great cold with potato salad or a cold pasta salad and corn on the cob.

COMPLETE NUTRITIONAL VALUES: **
Total Fat **11g** 17 % **(Sat Fat 1g** 5 %) Total Carbohydrates **59g** 20 % Fiber **12g** 48 % Sugars **4g** --- Cholesterol **0mg** 0 % Sodium **722mg** 30 % Protein **17g** 34 %

* (nutritional facts are per serving and accuracy is not certain)
** (percentages based on 2000 calories diet, data may be incomplete or calculations inaccurate)

Tofu stuffing

READY TO EAT IN: 30 min
MAKES: 8
GOOD STUFF 2 KNOWN: * Calories: **487** Total Fat: **42g** Cholesterol: **0mg**
SERVE FOR: Dinner

INGREDIENTS

2 8 ounce blocks tofu extra firm (drained and crumbled)
2 7 ounce bricks 5 grain tempeh (crumbled)
1 cup sweet onion (diced)
3 cups walnuts (chopped)
¼ cup cold pressed extra-virgin olive oil
½ cup white miso
¼ cup balsamic vinegar
3 ounces tomato paste
1 tablespoon thyme
1 teaspoon rosemary
1 teaspoon parsley

DIRECTIONS

In a large skillet saute onions, garlic, walnuts and tempeh in the olive oil. Stir frequently and cook for about 5 minutes. Crumble the tofu into the skillet and cook until dry but must remain tender.

Using a large mixing bowl combine the miso, vinegar, tomato paste and tahini and thoroughly mix the contents. Slowly add in the tofu-onion contents and continue to mix.

Season with the herbs and mix once again. Ready to serve.

MAKE IT BETTER:
Place into a crock pot with a mushroom gravy, cover and let cook for two hours on low heat.

GOES WELL WITH:
Lunch – Try a portabello mushroom sandwich and a dark greens salad with this.

Dinner – Serve with a brown rice vegan pilaf and a spinach salad .

COMPLETE NUTRITIONAL VALUES: **
Total Fat **42g** 65 % **(Sat Fat 5g 25 %)** Total Carbohydrates **18g** 6 % Fiber **5g** 20 %
Sugars **5g** --- Cholesterol **0mg** 0 % Sodium **733mg** 31 % Protein **16g** 32 %

* (nutritional facts are per serving and accuracy is not certain)
** **(**percentages based on 2000 calories diet, data may be incomplete or calculations inaccurate)

Sweet potato casserole

READY TO EAT IN: 40 min
MAKES: 6
GOOD STUFF 2 KNOWN: * Calories: **262** Total Fat: **10g** Cholesterol: **10mg**
SERVE FOR: Dinner

INGREDIENTS

6 medium sweet potatoes (cooked and peeled)
2 tablespoons vegan butter
½ cup dates
½ cup pecans
2 teaspoon vanilla extract
¼ cup soy milk
1 tablespoon pure maple syrup
¼ teaspoon sea salt
¼ teaspoon nutmeg (fresh if available)
1 teaspoon cinnamon

DIRECTIONS

Preheat the oven to 350° F. Spray a 2 quart casserole dish with non-stick spray or wipe with canola oil.
In a large mixing bowl mash the sweet potatoes with the vegan butter until smooth. Add the soy milk, vanilla, maple syrup, salt, nutmeg and cinnamon. Pour mixture into the prepared casserole dish.

Place the dates and pecans on top and bake for 25 minutes or until potatoes are firm and pecans are tender.

MAKE IT BETTER:
Blend one cup of pecans with a half of cup of dates and stir them into the sweet potato mixture instead of placing whole pieces on the top of it. Bake it until firm.

GOES WELL WITH:
Dinner – Any fake meat, a green salad and a tasty corn relish.

COMPLETE NUTRITIONAL VALUES: **
Total Fat **10g** 15 % **(Sat Fat 3g 15 %)** Total Carbohydrates **41g** 14 % Fiber **6g** 24 %
Sugars **17g** --- Cholesterol **10mg** 3 % Sodium **228mg** 10 % Protein **4g** 7 %

* (nutritional facts are per serving and accuracy is not certain)
** (percentages based on 2000 calories diet, data may be incomplete or calculations inaccurate)

Simple pumpkin soup

READY TO EAT IN: 40 min
MAKES: 6
GOOD STUFF 2 KNOWN: * Calories: **196** Total Fat: **9g** Cholesterol: **7mg**
SERVE FOR: Lunch or Dinner

INGREDIENTS

1 tablespoon olive oil
½ cup chopped onion
2 tablespoons curry powder
1 15 ounce can pumpkin puree

2 cups vegetable broth
2 tablespoons pure maple syrup
¼ cup pecan pieces
2 cups hazelnut milk (original)
¼ teaspoon black pepper

DIRECTIONS

Preheat the oven to 375° F. Heat the oil in a large pot over medium heat. Stir in 1 tablespoon of the curry powder and the pumpkin puree, then whisk in the broth until smooth. Add 1 tablespoon of the maple syrup and season to taste with pepper. Simmer for 10 minutes to allow flavors to develop, stirring occasionally.

In a small bowl, combine the pecan pieces with the remaining maple syrup and curry powder until pecan are thoroughly coated. Place the pecans in a small baking dish and bake until toasted (not burnt) about 10 minutes. Remove from oven and let cool.

Using a whisk add the hazelnut milk into the pot and set the heat on low. Whisk often and cook until soup is hot but do not boil. Remove from heat and serve with pecans on top.

MAKE IT BETTER:
Try adding in potato cubes and mushrooms while cooking it for a unique potato style soup.

GOES WELL WITH:

Lunch – Any sandwich, soft or grilled and a spinach salad.

Dinner – Mashed potatoes, a bean salad and a breaded fake chicken patty.

COMPLETE NUTRITIONAL VALUES: **
Total Fat **9g** 14 % **(Sat Fat 2g 10 %)** Total Carbohydrates **24g** 8 % Fiber **4g** 16 %
Sugars **11g** --- Cholesterol **7mg** 2 % Sodium **440mg** 18 % Protein **6g** 13 %

* (nutritional facts are per serving and accuracy is not certain)
** **(**percentages based on 2000 calories diet, data may be incomplete or calculations inaccurate)

CRANBERRIES and SQUASH

READY TO EAT IN: 80 min
MAKES: 6
GOOD STUFF 2 KNOWN: * Calories: **106** Total Fat: **5g** Cholesterol: **0mg**
SERVE FOR: Dinner

INGREDIENTS

4 cups butternut squash (peeled and cubed)
¾ cup cranberries (dried)
2 medium sweet onions (quartered then sliced)
¼ cup water

2 tablespoon extra-virgin olive oil
3 cloves garlic (chunks)
1 tablespoon oregano
1 teaspoon rosemary
   pinch black pepper
   pinch salt

DIRECTIONS

Preheat the oven to 350° F. Pour water over the cranberries and microwave for 30 seconds. Let them soak in the water. In a large mixing bowl combine all the ingredients except the cranberries. Drain cranberries and add to mix, and toss well. Pour into a rectangular glass baking dish and bake uncovered for 1 hour (or until the squash is tender to you liking). Add salt and pepper to taste at the table.

MAKE IT BETTER:
Try adding a small amount of a vegan red wine to the mix to enrich the combination of the sweet potatoes and cranberries.

GOES WELL WITH:
Dinner – Chicken fried tofu and green beans.

COMPLETE NUTRITIONAL VALUES: *
Total Fat **5g** 8 % **(Sat Fat 1g 5 %)** Total Carbohydrates **17g** 6 % Fiber **4g** 16 %

Sugars **4g** --- Cholesterol **0mg** 0 % Sodium **329mg** 14 % Protein **1g** 3 %

* (nutritional facts are per serving and accuracy is not certain)
** (percentages based on 2000 calories diet, data may be incomplete or calculations inaccurate)

Asparagus casserole

READY TO EAT IN: 60 min
MAKES: 6
GOOD STUFF 2 KNOWN: * Calories: **111** Total Fat: **3g** Cholesterol: **5mg**
SERVE FOR: Lunch, Dinner

INGREDIENTS

2 cups fresh asparagus
1 large yellow onion (thinly sliced)
8 ounces mushrooms (chopped)
2 cups parsnips (chopped)
3 cloves garlic (minced)
1 tablespoon vegan butter
¼ cup nutritional yeast
1 teaspoon sea salt (fine)
1½ cups water

DIRECTIONS

Preheat the oven to 350° F. Melt vegan butter in a large skillet and add the sliced onions. Saute gently over medium-low heat for about 45 minutes, stirring occasionally until caramelized. Use a splash of water, as needed, to prevent sticking. Once the onions are tender and golden in color, remove from heat and set aside in a bowl for later.

While the onions are cooking steam the parsnips. Fit a steamer basket into a saucepan, and fill with one inch of water. Add the parsnips and bring the water to boil over high heat. Cover and reduce the heat to low, steaming for about 8 minutes or until the parsnips are easily pierced with a fork. Transfer the steamed parsnips to your blender container and set it aside.

Drop fresh asparagus into boiling water. As soon as they turn bright green, remove them from the heat and plunge them into ice water. This will truncate the cooking process. Proceed with draining the water. Transfer the cooked asparagus into an 8" x 8" glass baking dish.

Once the onions have finished caramelizing, you can use the same pan to saute the mushrooms and garlic. Melt more butter and saute the garlic for about 3 minutes, then add the mushrooms. Cook for about 6 minutes or until liquid is released from the mushrooms.

Spread half of the mushroom mixture into the baking dish of asparagus and pour the other half of the mixture, along with any liquid, into the blender container with the steamed parsnips. Also add in the water, sea salt (to taste) and nutritional yeast. Blend until smooth and creamy.

Pour the creamy sauce over the asparagus and mushrooms in the glass baking dish, and stir to coat well.
Smooth the creamy vegetable mixture with a spatula, and top with the caramelized onions to finish.
Bake uncovered for about 30 minutes or until bubbly. Remove from oven and serve warm.

MAKE IT BETTER:
Top with your favorite fake cheddar cheese.

GOES WELL WITH:
Lunch – A vegan grilled fake cheese or fake meat sandwich, sweet potato fries and/or fresh fruit.

Dinner – Grill a fake chicken patty and a vegan potato salad. This is a perfect side dish for any meal including pasta, rice or even burritos.

COMPLETE NUTRITIONAL VALUES: **

Total Fat **3g** 5 % **(Sat Fat 1g 5 %)** Total Carbohydrates **18g** 6 % Fiber **7g** 28 %
Sugars **5g** --- Cholesterol **0mg** 0 % Sodium **424mg** 18 % Protein **7g** 14 %

* (nutritional facts are per serving and accuracy is not certain)
** **(**percentages based on 2000 calories diet, data may be incomplete or calculations inaccurate)

Pumpkin pudding

READY TO EAT IN: 100 min
MAKES: 6
GOOD STUFF 2 KNOWN: * Calories: **172** Total Fat: **2g** Cholesterol: **6mg**
SERVE FOR: Dessert

INGREDIENTS

1 15 ounce can pureed pumpkin
2 cups hazelnut milk (soy works fine)
3 tablespoons corn starch
2 tablespoons molasses
¼ cup brown sugar
½ teaspoon cinnamon
½ teaspoon nutmeg
½ teaspoon salt

DIRECTIONS

Whisk or blend together all ingredients until smooth and creamy.

Simmer over a medium to low heat for 8 minutes or until thickened.

Pour the mixture into individual serving cups and chill for about 90 minutes or until the pudding is set and firm.

Serve cold and enjoy.

MAKE IT BETTER:
Try sprinkling shredded coconut over finished pudding or serving with fake whipped cream.

GOES WELL WITH:
Dessert – A cup of hot apple cider.

COMPLETE NUTRITIONAL VALUES: *
Total Fat **2g** 3 % **(Sat Fat 1g 5 %)** Total Carbohydrates **36g** 12 % Fiber **5g** 20 %
Sugars **24g** --- Cholesterol **6mg** 2 % Sodium **252g** 11 % Protein **5g** 9 %

* (nutritional facts are per serving and accuracy is not certain)
** (percentages based on 2000 calories diet, data may be incomplete or calculations inaccurate)

Carrot muffins

READY TO EAT IN: 30 min
MAKES: 10
GOOD STUFF 2 KNOWN: * Calories: **105** Total Fat: **7g** Cholesterol: **16mg**
SERVE FOR: Dessert

INGREDIENTS

1 cup carrots (peeled then grated)
1 egg equivalent replacer
¼ cup raw sugar
¼ cup organic applesauce
½ teaspoon vanilla extract
¼ cup coconut oil
½ unbleached flour
1 teaspoon baking powder
½ teaspoon baking soda
2 teaspoons cinnamon
½ teaspoon salt

DIRECTIONS

Preheat the oven to 350° F. Grease a muffin tin. Place carrots in food processor and pulse a few times until they are grated. Add in the egg replacer, raw sugar, applesauce, vanilla and coconut oil then blend until well combined.

In a separate bowl, sift & mix together together all dry ingredients (flours, baking powder, baking soda, cinnamon and salt). Pour wet ingredients into the dry and gently fold together. Do Not over mix. Scoop batter into the greased muffin tin (about 1/3 of a cup batter per muffin.

Bake for 15 minutes or until done. Serve warm or cold.

MAKE IT BETTER:
Make a coconut whip topping by carefully opening a can of coconut milk and scooping off the thick solidified part on the top. (save the rest for another use). Whisk vigorously by hand (or in a mixer). Add two tablespoons of pure maple syrup to sweeten it up. Add a small scoop onto each muffin (once they are cooled off) and sprinkle with a dusting of cinnamon.

GOES WELL WITH:
Dessert – A cup of hot cider.

COMPLETE NUTRITIONAL VALUES: **
Total Fat **7g** 11 % **(Sat Fat 6g 30 %)** Total Carbohydrates **10g** 3 % Fiber **1g** 4 %
Sugars **7g** --- Cholesterol **16mg** 5 % Sodium **204mg** 9 % Protein **1g** 2 %

* (nutritional facts are per serving and accuracy is not certain)

** (percentages based on 2000 calories diet, data may be incomplete or calculations inaccurate)

Apple torte

READY TO EAT IN: 45 min
MAKES: 10
GOOD STUFF 2 KNOWN: * Calories: **319** Total Fat: **15g** Cholesterol: **90mg**
SERVE FOR: Dessert

INGREDIENTS

5 red apples (thinly sliced)
4 egg equivalent replacer
½ cup vegan butter (softened)
¾ cup raw sugar
½ cup almonds (sliced)
½ teaspoon baking powder
½ teaspoon baking soda
½ teaspoon cinnamon
1 tablespoon powdered raw sugar
1½ cups unbleached flour
2 tablespoons soy milk

DIRECTIONS

Preheat the oven to 400° F. Lightly grease a cake pan. Whisk together the vegan butter, raw sugar and egg replacer until well mixed. Add the flour and baking powder and stir thoroughly. Add the soy milk until the batter is smooth and creamy, adding more or less as needed.

Pour the batter into the cake pan. Gently place the apple slices on top of the batter, then sprinkle with the cinnamon and a little raw sugar.

Bake for 25 to 30 minutes or until a knife inserted in the center comes out clean.

Sprinkle the torte with powdered sugar then allow to cool. Serve warm.

MAKE IT BETTER:
Try drizzling the finished torte with real maple syrup.

GOES WELL WITH:
Dessert – A cup of hot coco and/or vegan ice cream.

COMPLETE NUTRITIONAL VALUES: **
Total Fat **15g** 23 % **(Sat Fat 7g 25 %)** Total Carbohydrates **43g** 14 % Fiber **3g** 12 %
Sugars **25g** --- Cholesterol **90mg** 30 % Sodium **154mg** 6 % Protein **6g** 12 %

* (nutritional facts are per serving and accuracy is not certain)
** (percentages based on 2000 calories diet, data may be incomplete or calculations inaccurate)

CPSIA information can be obtained
at www.ICGtesting.com
Printed in the USA
BVHW030326100922
646658BV00010B/660